GRAMMAR SONGS

Learning with Music

copyright 1984 by Kathy Troxel
revised - 1986, 1987, 1991, 1994

Published by
Audio Memory, Inc.
Newport Beach, CA
(800)365 - SING
www. audiomemory. com

words and music by Kathy Troxel

Cover design by Larry Troxel

all song arrangements and performances by Tim Smith
(except Verb Song 1, Capital Song, Direct Object Song)
guitar - Joe Cadrecha (Quotation Mark Song)

VOCALS

group singing - Eddie Vivero, Janet Vivero, Tim Smith, Kathy Troxel

solos - Rick Franz   Robert Olson   Tony Bowman
        (Sentence Song)   (Verb Song 2)   (Quotation Mark Song)

ACKNOWLEDGEMENTS

Special thanks to my husband, my family, fellow teachers,
many students and especially Tim Smith.

FOREWARD TO TEACHERS

The **Grammar Songs** book and tape have been prepared to supplement materials presently used in many schools throughout the nation. They provide students with a basic knowledge of grammar rules, punctuation rules and vocabulary. The music, rhythm, rhymes and pictures make the learning easier and more enjoyable. The students become totally involved in the subject by reading, hearing, singing and writing. They learn the material faster and retain it longer.

The material in this book was based on information from fifth through tenth grade grammar books. As you know, every year students review the parts of speech and rules of punctuation. First through tenth grade teachers are using **Grammar Songs** and adapting them as needed to their individual classroom situations.

Many of the songs contain information from the songs which precede them. For this reason, it is best to memorize them in order. Some songs such as the "Compound Personal Pronoun Drill" and the "Irregular Verb Drill" are only appropriate for those students who may be having difficulty in those areas (ESL students in particular).

Ideally each student should have his own tape and songbook to practice with at home. This speeds learning because the students teach themselves. It also motivates students to sing louder and to participate more readily with the class. The author has tested these songs with many classes and found that the best way to encourage the students to sing is to play a song several times and then tell them they may sing if they want to. You usually won't be able to stop them from singing. Offer a reward to the first student who can memorize the first verse or the whole song. That way, even if the students don't care for the music, they will appreciate the fact that it **does help them memorize.**

" A wise teacher makes learning a joy..." - Proverbs

These songs and exercises will help you to:

- memorize parts of speech
- memorize grammar rules
- speak correctly
- punctuate correctly
- write correctly
- increase vocabulary
- enjoy English

How to use this book:

1. Read through the lyrics before you listen to each song.
2. Look at the examples and the pictures.
3. Listen to the song several times.
4. Do the exercises that follow each song.
5. Correct your answers.
6. Sing along with the song over and over until you have it memorized.
7. Learn the songs in order. Many of the songs contain information from the songs which precede them.
8. Keep a record of your progress on the progress chart.

Printed in the United States of America. ISBN # 1-883028-05-1

TABLE of CONTENTS

racing

bouncing

training

skating

skiing

Verb Song 1

I'm **running, jumping, singing** - that's because I am a verb.
I'm **hopping, dancing, ringing** - that's because I am a verb.
I'm **coming, going, hitting, throwing,**
Humming, rowing, sitting, blowing,
Riding, hiding, gliding, sliding -
Because I'm a verb.
I'm a verb, verb, verb - I'm an action word.
So put me where the action is 'cause I'm an action word.

Sometimes I use a **helping verb** to help me make a phrase.
I can use these helping verbs in many different ways.
Like - **Will** you go? and **Should** we stay?
And **May** I throw? and **Does** he play?
And **Have** you seen it? **Did** he eat it? **Can** we have some more?
I'm a verb, verb, verb - I'm an action word.
So put me where the action is 'cause I'm an action word.

Sometimes when I am doing something, it is in my head.
The action isn't physical, it's in my mind instead.
Like **thinking, feeling, hoping, dreaming,**
Looking, resting, moping, scheming,
Estimating, calculating and **relating** too.
I'm a verb, verb, verb - I'm an action word.
So put me where the action is 'cause I'm an action word.

Sometimes I am a **linking verb** - a link between two words -
Like **shall be, will be, should be, would be, can be** and **could be**.
Linking verbs are commonly the forms of the verb "be."
Like **was** and **were, is** and **are, am, being** and **be** -
I'm a verb, verb, verb - I'm an action word.
So put me where the action is 'cause I'm an action word.

1

Verb Song 2

I'm **running, jumping, singing**
That's because I am a verb
I'm **hopping, dancing, ringing**
That's because I am a verb
I'm **coming, going hitting, throwing**
Humming, rowing, sitting, blowing
Riding, hiding, gliding, sliding
Because I'm a verb

Sometimes I use a **helping verb**
to help me make a phrase.
I can use these helping verbs
In many different ways.
Like - **Will** you go?
And - **Should** we stay?
And - **May** I throw?
And - **Does** he play?
And - **Have** you seen it?
Did he eat it? **Can** we have some more?

I'm a verb, verb, verb
I'm an action word
So put me where the action is
'Cause I'm an action word

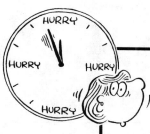

Sometimes when I am doing something,
It is in my head.
The action isn't physical,
It's in my mind instead -
Like **thinking, feeling, hoping, dreaming,
Looking, resting, moping, scheming,
Estimating, calculating and relating** too.

Sometimes I am a **linking verb**,
A link between two words -
Like **shall be, will be, should be,
Would be, can be** and **could be**
Linking verbs are commonly
The forms of the verb be -
Like **was** and **were, is** and **are
am, being** and **be.**

I'm a verb, verb, verb
I'm an action word
So put me where the action is
'Cause I'm an action word

3

Writing Exercise

Look at each picture on pages 6 and 7. Write as many verbs as you
can think of for each one. List them below.

1. _____

2. _____

3. _____

4. _____

5. _____

6. _____

7. _____

8. _____

9. _____

10. _____

11. _____

12. _____

13. _____

14. _____

15. _____

16. _____

Exercise 1

Underline the verbs in the following sentences. Underline the helping verbs too.

Example: You <u>will go.</u>

1. We should <u>stay</u> here until it gets dark.
2. You <u>may</u> give it to her when I <u>finish</u> with it.
3. He <u>will throw</u> it far across the field.
4. She <u>does play</u> piano better now than she did before.
5. Have you <u>seen</u> my picture in the paper?
6. They <u>did eat</u> breakfast before they left but they are hungry.
7. We can <u>have</u> some more ice cream if we want to.
8. She <u>has gone</u> downtown before, but she still gets lost.
9. You <u>could send</u> the package in the mail, but <u>call</u> first.
10. I <u>had already</u> seen the surprise, so I knew what to expect.

Exercise 2

Underline the verbs in the following sentences. Underline the linking verbs too.

Example: They <u>are coming</u> to the party.

1. He will <u>be sad</u> when his friend leaves.
2. They should <u>be here</u> before the bell rings.
3. That <u>would be</u> easy if I could open my locker.
4. I can <u>be</u> anything I want to be when I am in a costume.
5. Was that the first time you <u>lost</u> your homework?
6. Was he mad or does he always <u>yell</u> like that?
7. She is in the kitchen <u>studying</u> for finals.
8. I am too tired to <u>walk</u> another step.
9. He <u>is being</u> polite to the strangers.
10. Are you <u>coming</u> to my house or are you going to stay here?

Exercise 3   -   Underline all the verbs in the following paragraph.

Leroy has a job <u>mowing</u> lawns. Every Saturday, he <u>takes</u> his lawn mower around to his customers' homes. First he <u>rakes</u> the leaves. Then he <u>puts</u> them into a bag and he <u>picks</u> up the trash. He <u>mows</u> the lawn next. After he is <u>finished</u>, he <u>sweeps</u> up the cut grass. Sometimes he <u>feeds</u> the lawn with fertilizer. The customers <u>pay</u> him when he is <u>finished</u>. He <u>likes</u> his job a lot.

 9

10

 11

12

 13

14

 15

16

Noun Song

A person, a place or thing is a noun.
My **name** is a noun. **Fame** is a noun.
Everything I can be is a noun.
Everything I see is a noun.
Nouns can be **ideas** like **freedom** and **kindness**,
justice, **equality**, **sympathy** and **greatness**.

A person, a place or thing is a noun.
My **town** is a noun. **Clown** is a noun.
Everything I can be is a noun.
Everything I see is a noun.
Nouns are sometimes **proper** like **Lincoln** and **Texas**,
Honda, **Lake Michigan**, **Jennifer** and **Rome**.

A person, a place or thing is a noun.
Rain is a noun. **Plane** is a noun.
Everything I can be is a noun.
Everything I see is a noun.
Nouns are sometimes **common** like **city** or **country**,
county, **community**, **continent** or **tree**.

A person, a place or thing is a noun.
Mom is a noun. **Tom** is a noun.
Everything I can be is a noun.
Everything I see is a noun.

Abraham Lincoln was the *leader* of the
Union during the *Civil War.* He issued the
Emancipation Proclamation so that *slaves*
would have *freedom, justice* and *equality*.
He is known for his *kindness* and *greatness*.

Exercise 1

Circle the person, place, thing and idea nouns in each list below.

PERSON	PLACE	THING	IDEA
doctor	store	flashlight	pride
friend	park	piano	tree
alligator	mother	desk	pretty
child	wall	crying	easy
telephone	yard	enter	freedom
run	zoo	book	love
went	light	beside	bike
traffic	yellow	maybe	Chicago
also	floor	because	ice
nurse	cat	shirt	dreaming
stranger	flying	pants	greatness
man	over	guitar	lazy
rug	sky	after	looking
arm	library	happy	friendship
sister	brother	joyful	greed
fireman	Susan	money	big
coach	bedroom	under	slowly

compassion

charity

friendship

kindness

comfort

9

Writing Exercise

Look at each picture on pages 6 and 7. Write as many nouns as you can think of for each one.

Exercise 2 - VERB or NOUN?

In each sentence below, the underlined word is used as a noun or as a verb. If it is used as a noun, write N. If it is used as a verb, write V.

1. Running is good exercise. __N__
2. The dog is running through the park. __V__
3. Brush your teeth after every meal. __V__
4. He needs a new hair brush. __N__
5. The grass turned green after all that rain. __N__
6. It looks like it will rain today. __V__
7. He is going to check on the baby. __V__
8. Will that store accept your check? __N__
9. Do you love your brother? __V__
10. Love is very patient and kind. __N__
11. She is going to surprise him on his birthday. __V__
12. The surprise is hidden under the bed. __N__
13. That fly is a noisy pest. __N__
14. Don't you wish you could fly like a bird? __V__
15. He clowns around too much in our class. __V__
16. My favorite part of the circus is the clowns. __N__
17. Can you picture what this will look like? __V__
18. The picture is crooked. __N__
19. The race begins at 3:00. __N__
20. Do you want to race against me? __V__

Sentence Song

Every sentence has a subject and the subject does something
in the present, or the future or the past.
Every sentence has a subject and the subject does something
and remember that the period comes last.
It can be a question. It can be a statement.
It can also be an exclamation.

I see. - present   I will see. - future   I saw. - past

Exercise 1

A sentence which asks a question may begin with one of these words: *who*, *what*,
when, where, how, why, whose, does, to whom, is, are, were, was or *will*.
Put a question mark after every sentence which asks a question.

1. To whom should I send it
2. I like ice cream
3. How was summer camp
4. Get out of here
5. Where is my puppy

6. What time is it
7. Why are you leaving
8. She likes me
9. The skates go fast
10. When does school start

Exercise 2

A sentence which gives a command looks like it does not have a subject. The subject is understood. The subject is you. Write the word "you" before each command and say each sentence aloud with and without "you."

1. _You_ Sit down.
2. _You_ Look at that car.
3. _You_ Get out of here.
4. _You_ Leave me alone.
5. _You_ Help me.
6. _You_ Give me the keys.
7. _You_ Be quiet.
8. _You_ Listen to this.
9. _You_ Watch out.
10. _You_ Have fun.

Any of these commands can be said with strong feeling. Put an exclamation point after every command to show strong feeling.   !

Exercise 3 - FINDING SUBJECTS AND VERBS

1. Joseph baked a chocolate cake for the party.
   a. What is the action? _baked_ = VERB
   b. Who/what did the action? _Joseph_ = SUBJECT
2. Liz and Theresa have written a play together.
   a. What is the action ? _have written_ = VERB
   b. Who/what did the action ? _Liz + Theresa_ = SUBJECT
3. The musician practiced his pieces for two hours.
   a. What is the action? _practiced_ = VERB
   b. Who/what did the action? _musician_ = SUBJECT
4. Do they speak English very well?
   a. What is the action? _speak_ = _well_
   b. Who/what do the action? _They_ = _____
5. Corrie ten Boom hid Jewish people in her home in Holland.
   a. What is the action? _hid_ = _____
   b. Who/what did the action? _Corrie ten Boom_

Exercise 4 - TENSES

Read the following paragraph aloud 3 times. First read it in present tense, then past tense, then future tense.

It (is, was, will be) a gorgeous morning. The sun (shines, shone, will shine) brightly through the open window. I (can, could, will) smell pancakes and bacon cooking in the kitchen. As I (think, thought, will think) about the day ahead, I (start, started, will start) to get excited. There (is, was, will be) so much to do.

Writing Exercise

Look at each picture on pages 6 and 7. Write a sentence for each one using a noun as the subject, a linking verb and a verb.

Example: The boys are hiking.
          N   LV V

1. The _____ are _____ .

2. The _____ is _____ .

3. The _____ is _____ .

4. The _____ are _____ .

5. The _____ is _____ .

6. The _____ is _____ .

7. The _____ is _____ .

8. The _____ is _____ .

9. The _____ is _____ .

10. The _____ is _____ .

11. The _____ are _____ .

12. The _____ is _____ .

13. The _____ are _____ .

14. The _____ is _____ .

15. The _____ are _____ .

16. The _____ is _____ .

Pronoun Song

Pronouns take the place of nouns.
Pronouns take the place of nouns.
Pronouns take the place of nouns.
They take the place of nouns.

I and *me* and *us* and *we*
him and *her* and *it* and *she*
you and *they* and *them* and *he*
are personal pronouns

Pronouns are possessive when they show you that
something belongs to him or her or me.
Pronouns are possessive when they show you that
something belongs to someone.

This is *mine* and that is *yours*.
This is *his* and that is *hers*.
These are *ours* and those are *theirs*
and everybody owns something.

Rodney, Albert and Doug are on the football team.
They are on the football team.

Exercise 1 -   Fill in the blanks with the correct pronouns.

1. When is Mary coming?

    When is _____ coming?

2. Tom and David are my friends.

    _____ are my friends.

3. Mary and John are late.

    _____ and _____ are late.

4. The pie is delicious.

    _____ is delicious.

5. Give it to Karen and Tony.

    Give it to _____ .

I, you, he, she, it, we, they, me, him, her, my, mine, his, her, hers, your, yours, we, they, us, them, ours, our, their and *theirs* are all personal pronouns. Two of them joined by *and*, *or* or *nor* are called compound personal pronouns. People who never say, "Me went to the store," often say, "Sondra and me went to the store." The rule is to say compound personal pronouns the same way you would say them separately.

Example: Sondra went to the store. I went to the store.
          Sondra and I went to the store.

Exercise 2 -   Circle the letters of the correct sentences.

1. A. She and I are tired. B. Her and me are tired.
2. A. Him and I got there late. B. He and I got there late.
3. A. Are her and Brad coming? B. Are she and Brad coming?
4. A. Sandy and he are alike. B. Sandy and him are alike.
5. A. Him and her ran away. B. He and she ran away.
6. A. They and I are cousins. B. Them and me are cousins.
7. A. They and their dogs came. B. Them and their dogs came.
8. A. My friend and me went. B. My friend and I went.

Exercise 3 - Underline all the possessive pronouns in the following sentences.

1. The shoes are his.
2. The apples are theirs.
3. The book is yours.
4. Hers is the pink one.
5. Ours are the best.

6. The ring is mine.
7. Here is its cover.
8. The red bowl is hers.
9. The black one is ours.
10. Yours are bigger.

Exercise 4

The following words are some of the indefinite pronouns: **none, all, everyone, another, most, no one, someone, many, several** and **either**. Underline the indefinite pronouns in the following sentences.

1. Everyone was talking.
2. All of us are guilty.
3. Let's go another time.
4. Either one will work.
5. I like most of the boys.

6. No one can beat him.
7. Many came to the party.
8. Someone called Terry.
9. Several are missing.
10. None of us are ready.

Exercise 5

The following words are reflexive pronouns: **yourself, myself, himself, herself, ourselves, yourselves, themselves** and **itself**. Underline the reflexive pronouns in the following sentences.

1. John made himself lunch.
2. Joe laughed at himself.
3. Ann made it herself.
4. We stuffed ourselves with turkey.
5. They made themselves sick.

6. Make yourselves at home.
7. Do yourself a favor.
8. It opened by itself.
9. She acts like herself again.
10. I did not make it myself.

He is afraid to look at **himself**.

16

Compound Personal Pronoun Drill

Say it to her. Say it to me. Say it to her and me.
She and I hear you. Will she say it? Will I say it?
Will she and I say it over and over?

Say it to them. Say it to me. Say it to them and me.
They and I hear you. Will they say it? Will I say it?
Will they and I say it over and over?

Say it to him. Say it to us. Say it to him and us.
He and we hear you. Will he say it? Will we say it?
Will he and we say it over and over?

Say it to her. Say it to him. Say it to her and him.
She and he hear you. Will she say it? Will he say it?
Will he and she say it over and over?

Say it to Jim. Say it to us. Say it to Jim and us.
Jim and we hear you. Will Jim say it? Will we say it?
Will Jim and we say it over and over?

Say it to her. Say it to Kim. Say it to her and Kim.
She and Kim hear you. Will she say it? Will Kim say it?
Will she and Kim say it over and over?

Rule to remember: Never say, "Her and me are going."
She is going. + I am going. = She and I are going.

Personal pronouns joined by **and, or**, or **nor** are called compound personal pronouns.

She and I are going to play tennis.

Exercise 1

In the following sentences underline the correct one of the two pronouns in parentheses.

1. Please wait for him and (I, me).
2. Mary can't go without them and (I, me).
3. You walk next to (she, her) and (I, me).
4. The papers corrected by Lauren and (I, me) are missing.
5. The boy with him and (I, me) was Paul Cho.
6. (He, him) and (me, I) took a trip.
7. John and (I, me) are going to the ball game tonight.
8. Mark and Leslie are going with him and (I, me).
9. Jerry and (him, he) tried to hide the candy from Pat and (I, me).
10. They will call Matthew and (I, me) if they can go.
11. (They, them) and (me, I) earned enough money to go.
12. Rosalie invited (he, him) and (I, me) to the party.
13. Please help (she, her) and (I, me).
14. Are Tom and (I, me) late again?
15. They met Joshua and (we, us) at the banquet.
16. The teacher chose my friend and (I, me).
17. My friend and (I, me) are anxious to win.
18. (Her, she) and Kim live near (he, him) and (they, them).
19. Jim and (us, we) went to the basketball game.
20. We have a big surprise for (she, her) and (he, him).
21. He cooked dinner for (they, them) and (we, us).
22. (He, him) and (she, her) like Mexican food.
23. (She, her) and (he, him) visited us in the mountains.
24. Joe and (I, me) are going fishing.
25. Carl and (I, me) threw the pies at Sarah and (she, her).
26. Mr. Wilson offered money to Adam and (he, him).
27. Please tell Dad about (she, her) and (I, me).
28. They and (I, me) left after Mario and (her, she) left.
29. (Her, She) and (I, me) are going to ride horses.
30. Brian and (we, us) heard the good news from (she, her) and Kelly.

Adjective Song

SONG	EXAMPLE

Words that *modify nouns
and pronouns
telling which one
and what kind it is
or telling how many -
these are adjectives

many people
She looked **old**.
the **black** cat
silly girl
several hours
tiny baby

Words that modify nouns
and pronouns
telling which one
and what kind it is
or telling how many -
these are adjectives

yellow banana
He is **crazy**.
I like the **big, black** dog.
friendly doctor
three minutes

Simple and **easy** and **friendly** and **breezy** are adjectives.
Little and **tiny** and **middle** and **shiny** are adjectives.
Several and **few**, **older** and **new** are adjectives.
Costly and **cheap**, **purple** and **deep** are adjectives.

Words that modify nouns and pronouns, telling which one and what kind it is,
or telling how many - these are ADJECTIVES

Two birds flew into the
brilliant, **pink** sunset
between the **tall**, **swaying**,
palm trees. I felt the **cool**,
ocean breeze as I watched
the **gentle** waves lap the
white, **sandy** shore.

*Modify means describe or make definite.

Fill in the blanks with adjectives.

Grizzly bears are_____

and _____.

They have _____,

_____ coats.

Their ears are _____

and _____.

Their legs are _____

and _____.

Their eyes are _____

and _____.

The _____ moonlight is

shining on the _____,

_____ water.

_____ seagulls are flying

toward the _____,

_____ mountains.

The moon looks _____

and _____.

The _____ air smells

_____

and _____.

Writing Exercises

Look at each picture on pages 6 and 7. Write a sentence for each one using an adjective, a noun and a verb.

Example: The teenage boys are hiking.
           (adjective)(noun)   (verb)

1. The _____.

2. The _____.

3. The _____.

4. The _____.

5. The _____.

6. The _____.

7. The _____.

8. The _____.

9. The _____.

10. The _____.

11. The _____.

12. The _____.

13. The _____.

14. The _____.

15. The _____.

16. The _____.

Exercise 1

Modify means to make definite. Underline all the adjectives in the following sentences which make the nouns more definite.

1. There are <u>seventeen</u> people here.
2. The <u>black</u> cat hid under the <u>old</u> house.
3. The <u>silly</u> girl laughed at herself.
4. The <u>ferocious</u> dog barked at the <u>fearful</u> kitten.
5. We have only <u>three</u> minutes to get there.
6. This is an <u>easy</u> recipe for <u>chocolate</u> cake.
7. Chicago is the <u>windy</u> city.
8. The <u>tall</u>, <u>dark</u>, <u>handsome</u> stranger had a <u>friendly</u> smile and a <u>strong</u> handshake.
9. <u>Kind</u> words are like honey.
10. Be with <u>wise</u> people and become a <u>wise</u> person.

Exercise 2

Underline the adjectives in the following sentences which describe pronouns.

1. He is <u>crazy</u> and she is <u>adventurous.</u>
2. She is <u>silly</u> and <u>foolish</u>.
3. It is <u>simple</u>.
4. They are <u>old</u> and <u>experienced.</u>
5. We are <u>young</u> and <u>energetic.</u>
6. You look <u>tired</u> and <u>grumpy.</u>
7. It was hard to leave.
8. He is <u>stubborn</u> and <u>proud.</u>
9. She is <u>talkative</u> and vivacious.
10. They are <u>wealthy</u> and <u>generous.</u>

I like to be *different*.

Adverb Song

SONG	EXAMPLE

An adverb modifies a *verb*,
an *adjective*,
or another *adverb*.

march *slowly*
dead tired woman
rather slowly

An adverb modifies a *verb*,
an *adjective*,
or another *adverb*.

sing *loudly*
bitterly cold night
very quickly

It tells you *where*.
He does it *there*.
It tells you *when*.
He does it *then*.
It tells you *how*.
He does it *fast*.
To what *extent* -
He does it *all*.

It is *here*.
She walks *there*.
She is walking *now*.
She will walk *later*.
She walks *quietly*.
She walks *far*.
She walks *heavily*.
She sleeps *deeply*.

An adverb modifies a *verb*,
an *adjective*,
or another *adverb*.

hit *hard*
deep red curtains
somewhat softly

An adverb modifies a *verb*,
an *adjective*,
or another *adverb*.

speak *roughly*
rosy pink carpet
overly friendly

During the movie, Fred ate *quickly*, Mary cried *sadly*,
Ned slept *soundly*, and Ed laughed *heartily*.

Exercise 1

Underline the adverbs which modify verbs in the following sentences.

1. The band marches <u>quickly</u> in the pouring rain.
2. The choir sings <u>loudly</u> to be heard in the back.
3. In the deep jungle, the panthers run <u>swiftly</u>.
4. Please speak <u>clearly</u> so that I can hear you.
5. He hit the ball <u>hard</u> to the outfield.
6. The dessert will come <u>later</u>.
7. The magician performs <u>often</u>.
8. We searched <u>everywhere</u> for the lost puppy.

Exercise 2

Underline the adverbs which modify adjectives in the following sentences.

1. The <u>solid</u> gold Cadillac pulled up in front of us.
2. The sunset is <u>unusually</u> purple.
3. After the race, we were <u>thoroughly</u> exhausted.
4. He was <u>extremely</u> busy with his customers.
5. I am <u>dead</u> tired after shopping all day.
6. The <u>brilliant</u> blue water reflected the bright sun.
7. The <u>overly</u> protective mother clutched the child tightly.
8. The <u>partially</u> opened package was under the Christmas tree.

Exercise 3

Underline the adverbs which modify other adverbs in the following sentences.

1. He sings <u>very</u> beautifully.
2. I ate <u>too</u> quickly.
3. She slept <u>rather</u> soundly.
4. He came up to us <u>somewhat</u> cautiously.
5. They talk <u>too</u> slowly.
6. She drives <u>more</u> carefully since she got a ticket.
7. The sun shines <u>most</u> brightly at noon.
8. We breathe <u>less</u> easily in the smog.

He does it **all**.

24

Writing Exercise

Look at each picture on pages 6 and 7. Write a sentence for each one using an adjective, a noun a verb and an adverb.

Example: The teenage boys are hiking slowly.
          (adjective)(noun)   (verb) (adverb)

1. The _____.

2. The _____.

3. The _____.

4. The _____.

5. The _____.

6. The _____.

7. The _____.

8. The _____.

9. The _____.

10. The _____.

11. The _____.

12. The _____.

13. The _____.

14. The _____.

15. The _____.

16. The _____.

Apostrophe Song

SONG	EXAMPLE

I use an apostrophe
whenever I want to show
that someone owns something.
Then I can let them know
whose it is.

Jim's cat
Mary's car
Tom's watch
Jennifer's radio

If the noun is a proper name
ending in a **s**,
I add another **s**,
but just apostrophe is enough.

the Jones's house
the Jones' house
(either is correct)

If I leave out letters
when I write a word,
apostrophe in its place
is all you need to see.

'cause - because
'ritin' - writing
comin' - coming
'77 - 1977

Words like **yours** and **hers**,
ours and **theirs** and **its**,
don't need apostrophes
'Cause I already know whose it is.

The dog is hers.
Its cover is gone.
The ball is theirs.

I use an apostrophe
to put two words together
like **shouldn't**, **won't** and **she's**,
doesn't, didn't, that's,
I'm and **he's**.

should not - shouldn't
will not - won't
she is - she's
does not - doesn't
cannot - can't

If I leave out letters
when I write a word,
apostrophe in its place
is all you need to see.

'cept - except
cheatin' - cheating
runnin' 'round - running around

I use an apostrophe whenever I want to show that someone owns something.
Then I can let them know whose it is.

Rita's red hair   **Betty's** blonde hair   **Audrey's** auburn hair

Exercise 1

Put apostrophes wherever they are needed in the following sentences.

1. Jims car is in the garage.
2. Toms watch is broken.
3. Tanyas radio doesnt work.
4. The Adams house is across the street.
5. Shell be comin roun the mountain when she comes.
6. The bike is theirs.
7. You shouldnt do that.
8. Shes the best isnt she?
9. Where were you in 92?
10. Whats wrong with Lisas bike?
11. Its been a long time since its owner washed it.
12. Brads cassette is in its case.
13. Why wont they give them theirs?
14. Shes the owner and hes the manager.
15. Ritas long red hair is the same color as her mothers.

Mrs. Weiss' window

Gary's guitar

Rick's rake

Peter's puppet

Belinda's book

Mandy's microphone

Preposition Song

SONG

A preposition always
introduces a phrase.
A noun or pronoun always
comes at the end of that phrase.
Some prepositions are :
above, at, up and *down, through,*
underneath, until, against,
off, on and *onto.*

Come to me *at* the castle. I'll be waiting
in the dungeon, looking *out* the window.
Watch out *for* alligators.

Some prepositions are:
across, with, without and *from, to* -
concerning, over, under, by
for, with and *into.*
Some prepositions are:
before, after, during, like, on
around, below, along, beneath,
off, within, and *upon.*

You travel *up* the mountain, and go *beyond*
the vultures, *through* the scary forest.
Please rescue me *from* danger.

EXAMPLE

over the hill
around the corner
to her
with me
above the stairs
at the club
underneath the seat
off the wall
beside the door
across the street
with him
from my mother
into the garage
before the game
after the show
during the movie
along the side
through the window
by the river
down the hill
up the mountain
throughout the year
within the group
inside the pocket
behind the tree

Exercise 1

Underline the prepositions in the following sentences.

1. Come to me at the castle.
2. I'll be waiting in the dungeon.
3. We'll be looking out the window.
4. Watch out for alligators.
5. You travel up the mountain.
6. Go beyond the vultures.
7. Go through the scary forest.
8. Please rescue me from danger.
9. During the movie, the popcorn fell under the seat.
10. Before the game, the team went to the restaurant.
11. Look behind the garage and beneath the shelves.
12. The dog with the puppies is a poodle.
13. They get up early and work hard on the farm.
14. They stood in front of the class.
15. They lived across the street for many years.

Fill in the blanks.

A preposition always introduces a _____.

A _____ or _____ always comes at the end of that

_____.

Nick is almost *to* the top.
Leslie is **beneath** him.
Tyler is **under** her.
Lauren is **at** the end.
They started **in** the morning.
They finished **after** dark.
No one fell **off** the mountain.

Direct Object Song

The direct object receives the action from the verb.
The direct object receives the action from the verb.
The direct object receives the action from the verb.
Oh, the direct object (the direct object)
receives the action (receives the action) from the verb.

I hit _____. (whom or what)
I took _____. (whom or what)
I quit _____. (whom or what)
I shook _____. (whom or what)
I squeezed _____. (whom or what)
I loved _____. (whom or what)
I pleased _____. (whom or what)
I shoved _____. (whom or what)

Exercise 1 - Fill in the blanks of the song with direct objects.

DIRECT OBJECTS

I get the **fries**.
She ordered the **milk shake**.
He gets the **hamburger**.
You get the **hot dog**.

PREPOSITIONAL PHRASES

We're waiting **in the car.**
We're looking **at the food.**
The drinks are **on the top.**
She's waiting **for the cash.**

Exercise 2

The following sentences are related to the pictures on pages 6 and 7. Finish each one with either a direct object or a prepositional phrase. A prepositional phrase begins with a preposition.

1. The teenagers are hiking _____.
   (prepositional phrase)

2. The lady is running _____.
   (prepositional phrase)

3. The man is blowing out the _____.
   (direct object)

4. The choir is singing _____.
   (direct object)

5. The man threw the _____.
   (direct object)

6. The boy lit the _____.
   (direct object)

7. The man is wearing a _____.
   (direct object)

8. The girl is riding _____.
   (direct object)

9. The lady is sipping a _____.
   (direct object)

10. The man is freezing _____.
    (prepositional phrase)

11. Grandma is sharing the _____.
    (direct object)

12. The people are driving the _____.
    (direct object)

13. The group is listening _____.
    (prepositional phrase)

14. The boy is floating _____.
    (prepositional phrase)

15. The children are building a _____.
    (direct object)

16. The boy is riding a_____.
    (direct object)

Capital Song

first words in sentences
organizations
business firms
proper nouns
races
religions
government bodies and
special events
These are all things that are capitalized.
continents
countries
and counties
and cities
islands
and mountains
and bodies of water
heavenly bodies like
Saturn or Mars
These are all things that are capitalized.

EXAMPLE

He is very funny.
Lions Club, Elks Club
J.C. Penney
Abraham Lincoln, Colorado
Negro, Asian, Hebrew
Christian, Buddhist, Hindu
Supreme Court, Congress
World Series, Olympics

South America, Africa
Israel, Mexico
Orange County
Detroit, Paris
Easter Island, Patmos
Mt. Everest, Mt. Kilimanjaro
Pacific Ocean, Red Sea
Milky Way, Pluto

Statue of Liberty

New York City

World Trade Center

Empire State Building

Manhattan Island

Atlantic Ocean

Hudson River

32

SONG	EXAMPLE
calendar items like	St. Patrick's Day
Christmas and Easter	Yom Kippur
proper adjectives like	French perfume
Mexican sister	Spanish leather
sections of country like	the Middle West
North, South, East, West	New England
Capitalize them and you'll pass the test.	
God and Bible	
books and paintings	<u>Pilgrim's Progress</u>
	Mona Lisa
other works of art	Statue of Liberty
stories and	"The Cat in the Hat"
magazines	<u>Life, Time, People</u>
movies and	"The Sound of Music"
poems	"The Road Not Taken"
are CAPITALIZED	

<u>C</u>hristmas

<u>S</u>ilent <u>N</u>ight

NATIONALITIES

Mexican
Spanish
Canadian
Cuban
Iranian
French
German
Welsh
Thai
Indian
Israeli
Norwegian
Ethiopian

Exercise 1

Underline every word that should be capitalized.

1. i saw the washington monument and the lincoln memorial.
2. she gave me a necklace made of mexican silver.
3. you can get danish pastry in solvang.
4. before i was a christian, i was a hindu.
5. the channel islands are near santa barbara.
6. in southeast asia there is malaysia.
7. when i was in new york, i saw the statue of liberty.
8. the smallest continent, australia, is between the indian and the pacific oceans.
9. one of the new england states is massachusetts.
10. two holidays which are very close are easter and passover.
11. the next olympics will be held in seoul, korea.
12. the civil war was between the north and the south.
13. "it's a wonderful life" is a classic christmas movie.
14. for the chinese, this is the year of the dragon.
15. my aunt carmen gets national geographic magazine.
16. the president spoke with protestant, catholic and jewish leaders at a private meeting in the white house.
17. to kill a mockingbird is a novel about life in a small town in maycomb county, alabama.
18. the junior prom comes right after the winter carnival.
19. i play my favorite sport, volleyball, in the summer.
20. my uncle is caucasian and my aunt is latin.
21. we have a chevrolet, a volkswagen and a ford.
22. our high school play this year is "fiddler on the roof."
23. our two main political parties are the democrats and the republicans.
24. the queen of england missed the opening of parliament.
25. The first ten amendments to the constitution are called the bill of rights.

Irregular Verb Drill

INFINITIVE	PRESENT PARTICIPLE	PAST	PAST PARTICIPLE
blow	blowing	blew	have blown
throw	throwing	threw	have thrown
fly	flying	flew	have flown
grow	growing	grew	have grown
fight	fighting	fought	have fought
bring	bringing	brought	have brought
buy	buying	bought	have bought
seek	seeking	sought	have sought
teach	teaching	taught	have taught
catch	catching	caught	have caught
take	taking	took	have taken
shake	shaking	shook	have shaken
drink	drinking	drank	have drunk
shrink	shrinking	shrank	have shrunk
stink	stinking	stank	have stunk
sink	sinking	sank	have sunk
feed	feeding	fed	have fed
flee	fleeing	fled	have fled
lead	leading	led	have led
bleed	bleeding	bled	have bled
sting	stinging	stung	have stung
hang	hanging	hung	have hung
sing	singing	sang	have sung
ring	ringing	rang	have rung

Will the boat sink?

The boat is sinking.

The boat just sank.

They have sunk.

INFINITIVE	PRESENT PARTICIPLE	PAST	PAST PARTICIPLE
strive	striving	strove	have striven
drive	driving	drove	have driven
give	giving	gave	have given
dive	diving	dove	have dived
burn	burning	burnt	have burned
burst	bursting	burst	have burst
bear	bearing	bore	have borne
tear	tearing	tore	have torn
come	coming	came	have come
break	breaking	broke	have broken
go	going	went	have gone
speak	speaking	spoke	have spoken
sit	sitting	sat	have sat
slay	slaying	slew	have slain
stand	standing	stood	have stood
know	knowing	knew	have known
bind	binding	bound	have bound
wind	winding	wound	have wound
hear	hearing	heard	have heard
find	finding	found	have found
get	getting	got	have gotten
do	doing	did	have done
shine	shining	shone	have shined
win	winning	won	have won

The wind blew.

The water ran.   The girl drank.

INFINITIVE	PRESENT PARTICIPLE	PAST	PAST PARTICIPLE
send	sending	sent	have sent
swim	swimming	swam	have swum
bid	bidding	bid	have bid
run	running	ran	have run
rise	rising	rose	have risen
ride	riding	rode	have ridden
freeze	freezing	froze	have frozen
choose	choosing	chose	have chosen
hide	hiding	hid	have hidden
slide	sliding	slid	have slid
rid	ridding	rid	have rid
do	doing	did	have done
light	lighting	lit	have lit
bite	biting	bit	have bitten
slit	slitting	slit	have slit
quit	quitting	quit	have quit
stick	sticking	stuck	have stuck
strike	striking	struck	have struck
give	giving	gave	have given
sneak	sneaking	snuck	have snuck

I want to hit the ball.
I am hitting the ball.
I hit the ball yesterday.
I have hit the ball before.

Exercise 1

Write the past tense of each verb in the following sentences.

1. (ring) He _____ the bell several times.
2. (fight) The dogs _____ in the alley.
3. (shake) I _____ the rug as hard as I could.
4. (buy) They _____ a newspaper.
5. (sting) The bee _____ me this morning.
6. (sing) They _____ carols to the neighbors.
7. (bleed) He _____ all over the seat.
8. (slay) David _____ Goliath, the giant.
9. (drive) We _____ many miles to get here.
10. (dive) He _____ into the deep pool.
11. (flee) They _____from the enemy army.
12. (sink) The "unsinkable" Titanic _____.
13. (hang) The clothes _____ on the line in the rain.
14. (shrink) My sweater _____ when I washed it.
15. (drink) He _____ a quart of milk.
16. (feed) Have you _____ the bears?
17. (lead) She _____ us through the museum.
18. (swim) They _____ across the channel.
19. (strike) He _____ the match on the sidewalk.
20. (bite) The cat _____ the fish.
21. (break) They _____ through the window.
22. (strive) I _____ to win the championship.
23. (hear) We _____ about it on the news.
24. (speak) I _____ with your parents.
25. (seek) They _____ for the lost child.
26. (bind) Samson broke the ropes that _____ him.
27. (stand) We _____ in line for an hour.
28. (wear) Alex _____ his new uniform to work.
29. (tear) The dog _____ the magazine apart.
30. (catch) The catcher _____ the fast ball.
31. (teach) My father _____ me how to drive.
32. (shine) The car _____ brightly after we washed it.
33. (freeze) The meat _____ in the freezer.

Plural Song

To form a plural when a word ends in **y**,
you change the **y** to **i** and add **es** -
like **spy** into **spies** and **fly** into **flies**,
enemy to **enemies** and **cry** to **cries**

To form a plural when the word ends in **y**,
after a vowel then you add an **s** -
like **day** into **days** and **play** into **plays**,
turkey into **turkeys**, **holiday** - **holidays**

Words used for music that end in an **o** -
you form the plural when you add an **s** -
soprano - **sopranos** and **alto** to **altos**,
piano to **pianos** and **solo** to **solos**.

The plural of some nouns is irregular.
If you remember these you'll be a star -
tooth into **teeth**, **mouse** into **mice**,
ox to **oxen**, **child** to **children**, **woman** - **women**

Sometimes the plural is the singular.
If you remember these you'll really go far -
like **deer** into **deer**, **sheep** into **sheep**,
salmon - **salmon**, **fish** to **fish**, **Chinese** to **Chinese**.

To form a plural when a word ends in **o**,
when there's a consonant before the **o**,
you add an **es**, like changing **hero** to **heroes**,
potato to **potatoes** and **tomato** - **tomatoes**.

When you have words that end in **ch** or **x**,
z, **sh** or **s**, then you add **es** -
like **box** into **boxes**, and **fox** into **foxes**,
rich to **riches**, **miss** to **misses**, **kiss** to **kisses**.

There are some words that end in **f** or **fe**.
The plural of the words changes these -
like **leaf** into **leaves**, **knife** into **knives**,
wolf to **wolves**, **self** to **selves** and **life** to **lives**.

puppy - puppies

child - children

butterfly - butterflies

39

Exercise 1

Write the plural form of the following words.

1. leaf

2. box

3. piano

4. knife

5. potato

6. wolf

7. enemy

8. fly

9. mouse

10. self

11. foot

12. tooth

13. wife

14. woman

15. ox

16. child

17. tomato

18. self

19. soprano

20. hero

21. spy

22. half

23. shelf

24. solo

25. life

26. lady

27. church

28. city

29. thief

30. brush

one leaf

many leaves

Comma Song

Use a comma to separate items in a series
if they're not joined by **and** or **or**.

You usually separate independent clauses
in a series by semi-colons.

Use a comma to separate two or more adjectives
if they come before a noun.

When you join independent clauses, use a comma before:
and, but, or, nor, for and **yet**.

Words used in direct address - use a comma.
Appositive, appositive phrases - use a comma.
Parenthetical expressions - use a comma too.

Use a comma to separate short independent clauses.
That'll make it look all right.

Use a comma for non-essential clauses and phrases.
That'll help you do it right.

Words used in direct address - use a comma.
Appositive, appositive phrases - use a comma.
Parenthetical expressions - use a comma too.

Use a comma to separate items in addresses
and to separate the items in dates.

And at the ending of a letter when you sign it with love -
that'll help you keep your mate.

Words used in direct address - use a comma.
Appositive, appositive phrases - use a comma.
Parenthetical expressions - use a comma too.

Herbie, Violet and Curtis are jumping for joy.

ITEMS IN A SERIES

Think of the World Series. It is a group of games played one after the other. "Items in a series" means a list of things written one after the other.

Example: We ate apples, oranges, bananas and pears.

Rule: Use a comma to separate items in a series.

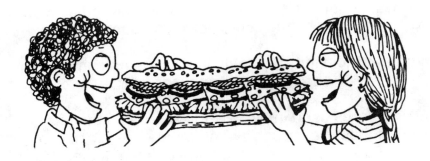

The sandwich has onions, tomatoes, pickles, lettuce, cheese, turkey, peppers and salami.

SEMICOLON

A semicolon (;) is used to join two independent clauses together.

Example: Jeff tried to start the car; there was no gas.

A semicolon is used to join two independent clauses together when they are connected by words such as: *also, however, furthermore, instead, as a result, besides, meanwhile, for example* and *then*.

Example: We made plans to arrive early, get a good seat and enjoy the show; instead, we got there late, sat in the back and missed the beginning.

A semicolon is used to separate groups of words which contain commas.

Example: I went to the dentist on the following dates: Feb. 1, 1989; May 11, 1989; March 5, 1990; and July 9, 1991.

Example: We lived in the following capital cities: Albany, New York; Lansing, Michigan; Columbus, Ohio; Jackson, Mississippi; Indianapolis, Indiana; Springfield, Illinois and Cheyenne, Wyoming.

CLAUSE

A clause is a group of words which has a subject and a verb and which is used as part of a sentence. If that part of the sentence can make a sentence by itself, it is called an **independent** clause. If it cannot make a sentence by itself, it is called a **dependent** clause.

Rule: When you join independent clauses use a comma before: **and, but, or, nor, for** and **yet**.

A dependent clause **cannot** stand by itself.

An independent clause **can** stand by itself.

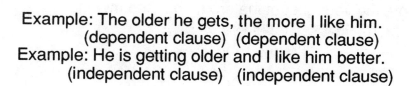

Example: The older he gets, the more I like him.
       (dependent clause) (dependent clause)
Example: He is getting older and I like him better.
      (independent clause)   (independent clause)

Rule: Separate independent clauses by semicolons. (;)

Example: The man opened the door; he walked into the room; he sat down quietly.

ADVERB CLAUSES

An adverb clause can come at the beginning of the sentence. It tells **where, when, how** or **to what extent**. Use a comma after an adverb clause.

Example: Before the fight, the heavyweight was awake all night.
In the dark, he sat and waited for the morning light.

APPOSITIVES

An appositive is a word or phrase within a sentence that follows a noun and tells something about it.

Example: Her friend Marty, **the club president**, was late.
(appositive phrase)
A friend from school, **Shelly**, is coming over later.
(appositive)

Note:
A group of words that begins with **who** or **which** is not an appositive but a clause. It contains a subject and a verb. An appositive does not.

Example: Her friend Marty, **who is the club president**, was late.
(clause)
That blue car, **which is my favorite**, is the most expensive.
(clause)

NON - ESSENTIAL CLAUSES

A non-essential clause does not have to be in the sentence.

Rule: Use a comma for non-essential clauses and phrases.

Example: Jim Gomez, who lives across the street, just graduated.
(non-essential clause)
He and I, the youngest of the group, had the most fun.
(non-essential clause)

Exercise 1

In the following sentences, use a comma to separate items in a series if they're not joined by **and** or **or**.

1. Capitalize races nationalities languages and religions.
2. Capitalize days of the week months holidays and street names.
3. He likes hunting and fishing and skiing and skating.
4. Capitalize political parties and state names and holidays.
5. Afro-American Caucasian Hispanic Indian and Asian are capitalized.

Exercise 2

In the following sentences, separate independent clauses in a series by semicolons.

1. The man opened the door he walked into the room he sat down slowly.
2. It was a foggy morning outside my mind was foggy too I went back to sleep.
3. Listen to me don't lose your courage don't ever think of giving up.
4. He came he saw he conquered.
5. We work hard we play hard we sleep deeply.

Exercise 3

In the following sentences, use commas to separate adjectives when they come before a noun.

1. He drove a large shiny blue convertible.
2. He pinned a single red rose to his wide white lapel.
3. The missing boy is wearing a filthy torn green shirt.
4. They found the lost frightened kitten in the dark musty basement.
5. Small shiny green leaves are sprouting on the rare fragrant plant.

"He's covered with sticky,

smelly, red paint!"

Exercise 4

In the following sentences, use commas to join independent clauses before these words: and, but, or, nor, for and yet.

1. She went to the doctor but he couldn't find anything wrong.
2. I sent the money and I expect to receive the package soon.
3. The hot water was soothing yet I wanted to leave.
4. You can go with us or you can stay at home.
5. They had to go for the bus was waiting.

Exercise 5

"Direct address" means speaking to a person/people by name. Words used in direct address use a comma. Put commas after these in the following sentences.

Example: Lori, sit down.   Children, come here.

1. James I want to talk to you.
2. Suzanne please call me.
3. Margie let's go.
4. Nurse I need help.
5. Mark I miss you.

Exercise 6

In the following sentences, use commas for appositives and appositive phrases.

1. The party a surprise for Tammy was a success.
2. Bill the speaker was very inspirational.
3. My best friend Larry calls me every day.
4. Their new neighbor Shawn is a doctor.
5. Tyler the new baby grew strong and healthy.

"Harry Roberts, our guest speaker, has an important message."

Exercise 7

In the following sentences, use commas to separate short independent clauses.

1. We got up we got dressed we grabbed breakfast and we ran.
2. They came they saw and they conquered.
3. He skis he writes he sings he draws and he rests.
4. His tail is white his ears are white and his legs are white.
5. Take aspirin drink liquids go to bed and call me in the morning.
6. Be honest be fair be kind and forgive him.

Exercise 8

In the following sentences, use commas for parenthetical expressions.

1. The book in his opinion was full of lies.
2. The movie according to her was better than the play.
3. The hostages I hope are returning today.
4. She of course has been waiting patiently.
5. The documentary on the other hand was very factual.
6. The answer if you must know is in the back of the book.

Exercise 9

Use commas to separate items in the following addresses and dates.

1. Their address is 1445 W. Adams Blvd. Los Angeles Calif.
2. Their home is located at 228 Shoreline Drive Savannah Georgia.
3. He was born on July 28 1983 and she was born on May 4 1986.
4. His address on May 7 1954 was 1600 Pennsylvania Ave. Washington D.C.
5. In June 1990 we moved from Topeka Kansas to Lincoln Nebraska .
6. She called on Friday August 9 1991 and Thursday August 15 1991.

I woke up depressed,
but I decided to be happy.

47

Quotation Mark Song

Quotation marks go before the sentence said
and after the sentence to show what someone said.
Quotation marks go after the period or after the comma,
the question or the exclamation.

When a quoted sentence is interrupted
by an interruption like "he said" or "she said,"
quotation marks enclose the part of what is said.
Inside the quotations use commas when it's interrupted.

Quotation marks go before the sentence said
and after the sentence to show what someone said.
Quotation marks go after the period, or after the comma,
the question or the exclamation.

When you have a conversation between two or more people,
each time the speaker changes, you indent what they said.

Quotation marks go before the sentence said
and after the sentence to show what someone said.
Quotation marks go after the period, or after the comma,
the question or the exclamation.

Sometimes a quotation's inside another quote.
If this should ever happen, you use a single quote.
Use a single quote inside a double quote.
That way we can tell if he said, "She said, 'It's over.' "

Quotation marks enclose the titles of short stories,
poems, songs and chapters, articles and slang words.
Quotation marks enclose the titles of short stories,
poems, songs and chapters, articles and slang words.

Quotation marks go before the sentence said
and after the sentence to show what someone said.
Quotation marks go after the period, or after the comma,
the question or the exclamation.

" I really like you," he announced.
"Are you sure?" she asked.
"Yes I am!" he replied.
"That makes me so happy,"she said,"because I've been watching you for a long time."

Exercise 1

Put quotation marks where they belong in the following sentences. Write in the proper punctuation for the end of each sentence. Put quotation marks after periods, commas, question marks and exclamation points.

1. It is better he said if I leave early
2. Are you coming with us she asked or are you staying home
3. I hate messes she yelled
4. When is the movie going to start he asked
5. I really don't know he said what I want to do with my life
6. She said It's a good thing that we wore our jackets
7. Are you going to eat with us she asked or will you eat after the game
8. They screamed Fire! Fire! as loud as they could
9. If you do that again he roared you're fired
10. She exclaimed I found it at last

That's a "bad" car. - slang word
"The Cat in the Hat" - short story
"My Favorite Things" - song
"The New Beginning - episode in a television series
"The Raven" - poem
"I Am Joe's Heart" - magazine article

Exercise 2

In the following sentences use quotation marks to enclose the titles of short stories, poems, songs, chapters, articles, slang words and television episodes.

1. My favorite song is Climb Every Mountain.
2. Last year I read Hope for the Flowers, a short story by Trina Paulus.
3. He thinks it's cool to wear sunglasses at night.
4. Our assignment is to read the chapter titled Darkness in the book <u>A Tale of Two Cities.</u>
5. Chicago is a poem by Carl Sandburg.
6. There is a controversial article in the local newspaper titled, Taxation Without Representation.
7. This is the last episode of All Creatures Great and Small.
8. The Star Spangled Banner is our national anthem.
9. The poem he wrote is titled Dances with Lions.
10. He wears his hair like that because he wants to be rad.

Exercise 3

Sometimes a quotation is inside another quote. Use a single quote inside a double quote. Put single (') and double (") quotes where they belong in the following sentences.

1. He said, I never read The Night the Bed Fell. It's a short story.
2. Do you ever watch Little House on the Prairie ? she asked.
3. She asked, What poem begins with this line? Whose woods these are I think I know.
4. She said, I can't wait to see what happens on Another Life.
5. He said, She said, It's over.
6. He said, That shirt is rad, groovy and cool.
7. Will you sing Sunrise, Sunset at my wedding? she asked.
8. He announced, The Oscar winner is Dances With Wolves.
9. She said, His exact words were, Give me liberty or give me death.
10. He asked, Do you know the second verse of America the Beautiful?

Exercise 4

When you have a conversation between two or more people you have a dialogue. Each time the speaker changes, you indent the sentence. Put an arrow in front of each sentence which should be indented.

Example:

> She asked, "Would you rather give a gift or receive a gift?"
> "I'd rather give," he said, "because it's more fun. It makes me feel good.
   Besides, I already have everything I want."

Tom said, "Let's go to the basketball game tonight. Then afterwards we can go out for pizza and play some video games."
"I don't have any money for that," said Albert. "I'm saving up to go to camp."
"Why do you want to go to camp?" Tom asked.
"Haven't you ever been to camp? It's really fun!" Albert answered.
Tom said, "I'd rather spend my money now. I don't like to save it. Don't you have a lawn you could mow before tonight?"
"Maybe I can," Albert said. "I'll ask the Thompsons."

Greek & Latin Prefix & Suffix Song

2

```
    heat - thermo
    life - bio
    homo - same
  before - pro (pre)
   mater - mother
   pater - father
    post - after
    ject - throw
    ante - before
      ab - away from
   inter - between
   inter - within
```

Let's call the whole thing off!

1

```
     mis - wrong
  astron - star
 against - ob
  remain - sed
    crat - rule
 without - an
    onym - name
   capit - head
     com - together
     con - together
     col - together
   meter - measure
```

Let's call the whole thing off!

3

```
   frater - brother
       ex - out
  far off - tele
      see - scope
    psych - mind
   circum - around
    dynam - power
     greg - group
    gress - move
      all - pan
      iso - equal
  anthrop - man
```

Let's call the whole thing off!

4

```
    med - middle
   port - carry
  graph - write
  phone - sound
  again - re
  apart - se
 before - pre
    vid - see
   poly - many
   mono - one
   bene - well
  philo - love
```

5

```
 against - contra
    dict - say
 against - anti
    from - de
     God - theo
   world - cosmo
   false - pseudo
   earth - ge
   macro - large
   micro - small
    manu - hand
   order - mand
```

Let's call the whole thing off!

6

```
    soph - wise
    arch - chief
  beyond - extra
      bi - two
    self - auto
    cide - kill
  around - peri
     per - through
   hydra - water
    aqua - water
    semi - half
    hemi - half
```

Let's call the whole thing off!

Definitions

1. mis - wrong

 misbehave - use wrong behavior (v.)

 misprint - wrong printing

 misunderstand - have a wrong understanding (v.)

2. astron - star

 astronomy - study of the stars (n.)

 astronaut - someone who travels around the stars (n.)

 astrology - study of how the stars might affect people (n.)

3. against - ob

 object - speak against (v.)

 obstacle - something which goes against progress (n.)

 obstinate - rebellious against something / someone (adj.)

4. remain - sed

 sedentary - remaining in one place (adj.)

 sedated - drugged to remain calm (adj.)

 sedative - a drug which causes a person to remain calm (n.)

5. crat - rule

 theocrat - one who believes that God rules (n.)

 democrat - one who believes that people rule (n.)

 autocrat - one who believes you rule yourself (n.)

6. without - an

 anarchy - without a chief, without a ruler (n.)

 anaerobic - without oxygen (adj.)

 anonymous - without a name (adj.)

7. onym - name

 homonym - same name (n.)

 antonym - opposite name (n.)

 pseudonym - false name (n.)

8. capit - head

 capital - head city (n.)

 decapitate - cut off the head (v.)

 capitol - head government building (n.)

9. com - together

 commune - live together (v.)

 combine - put together (v.)

 compact - squeezed together (adj.)

10. con - together

 congregate - group together (v.)

 converge - come together (v.)

 connect - join together (v.)

11. col - together

 collect - gather together (v.)

 colony - a group living together (n.)

 collaborate - work together (v.)

12. meter - measure

 thermometer - measure of heat (n.)

 barometer - measures atmospheric pressure (n.)

 speedometer - measures speed (n.)

13. heat - thermo

thermal underwear - keeps in body heat (adj. - n.)
thermos - keeps in liquid heat (n.)
thermodynamics - power of heat (n.)

14. life - bio

biology - study of life (n.)
biography - written life story (n.)
autobiography - self-written life story (n.)

15. homo - same

homogenized - the same throughout (adj.)
homosexual - attracted to the same sex (adj.)
homographs - words written the same (n.)

16. before - pro

provide - give something before it is needed (n.)
prophecy - knowledge before of what will happen (n.)
promise - vow to do something before it is done (v.)

17. mater - mother

maternity - related to motherhood (adj.)
maternal - motherly (adj.)
matriarch - a woman who rules a family (n.)

18. pater - father

paternity - related to fatherhood (adj.)
paternal - fatherly (adj.)
patriarch - a man who rules a family (n.)

19. post - after

postpone - change date to a later date (v.)
post date - date after the real date (v.)
post script - written after the close of a letter (n.)
post-war - after the war (adj.)
postlude - music played afterwards (n.)
posterity - those who follow in later generations (n.)
posthumous - after death (adj.)

20. ject - throw

reject - throw away (v.)
eject - throw out (v.)
projectile - something that is thrown (n.)

21. ante- before

antebellum - before the Civil War (adj.)
antediluvian - before the Flood (adj.)
antedate - come before in time (v.)

22. ab - away from

abduct - carry away from (v.)
abnormal - away from normal (adj.)
abolish - take away (v.)
aberrant - away from normal (adj.)
abandon - go away from (v.)

23. inter - between

intervene - come between (v.)
international - between nations (adj.)
interrupt - break between (v.)
intercity - between cities (adj.)
interval - distance between two notes (n.)

24. inter - within

interior - within the inside (adj.)
internal - on the inside (adj.)

25. frater - brother

 fraternity - organization for brothers (n.)
 fraternal - brotherly (adj.)
 fraternize - act as brothers (v.)

26. ex - out

 exit - go out (v.)
 expire - breathe out (v.)
 explode - burst out (v.)
 expectorate -spite out (v.)
 exorcise - drive out evil spirits (v.)
 exterior - outside (n.)
 extinct - died out (adj.)
 extinguish - put out (v.)
 extract - pull out (v.)
 expel - push out (v.)
 extra - terrestrial - outside the earth (adj.)

27. far off - tele

 telegraph - write far off (v.)
 television - transmits pictures from far off (n.)
 telescope - instrument for seeing far off (n.)
 telephone - transmits sounds from far off (n.)

28. see - scope

 telescope - used to see far off (n.)
 periscope - used to see around (n.)
 microscope - used to see small things (n.)

29. psych - mind

 psychiatry - healing of the mind (n.)
 psyche - mind or soul (n.)
 psychology - study of the mind (n.)

30. circum- around

 circumference - measure around a circle (n.)
 circumscribe - draw a line around (n.)
 circumvent - surround (v.)

31. dynam - power

 dynamite - powerful destroyer (n.)
 dynamo - source of power (n.)
 dynasty - powerful family (n.)

32. greg - group

 congregate - group together (v.)
 aggregate - a group of different things (n.)
 gregarious - enjoys being in a group (adj.)

33. gress - move

 progress - move forward (v.)
 aggressive - moving towards (adj.)
 digress - stray from the subject (v.)

34. all - pan

 panacea - cure - all (n.)
 panorama - view of all things (n.)
 pandemic - affecting all things (adj.)

35. iso - equal

 isoceles triangle - has equal sides (adj.)
 isogonic - having equal angles (adj.)
 isothermal - having equal temperatures (adj.)

36. anthrop - man

anthropology - study of mankind (n.)
philanthropist - lover of mankind (n.)
anthropogenesis - beginning of man (n.)

37. med - middle

medium - in the middle (adj.)
mediator - person who acts in the middle (n.)
mediocre - not the best or worst, the middle (adj.)

38. port - carry

transport - carry across (v.)
portable - able to be carried (adj.)
import - carry in (v.)

39. graph - write

graphology - study of handwriting (n.)
autograph - self - written name (n.)
lithography - process of printing writing (n.)

40. phone - sound

telephone - brings sound from far off (n.)
earphone - puts sound in the ear (n.)
microphone - enlarges a small sound (n.)
phonics - system of learning by sound (n.)

41. again - re

return - go back again (v.)
reunite - unite again (v.)
reborn - born again (adj.)

42. apart - se

secluded - set apart (adj.)
secede - move apart from something (v.)
separate - apart (adj.)

43. before - pre

preview - see before (v.)
precede - come before (v.)
prediction - something said before (n.)

44. vid - see

video cassette - records thing to be seen (n.)
video games - seen on a screen (n.)
visual - able to be seen (adj.)

45. poly - many

polygamy - having many wives (n.)
polytheism - belief in many gods (n.)
monopoly - one owns many (n.)

46. mono - one

monogamy - having one wife (n.)
monologue - one person talks (n.)
monotheism - belief in one God (n.)

47. bene - well

benefit - do well for (v.)
benediction - speech of well - being (n.)
benevolent - treating well (adj.)

48. philo - love

philosophy - love of wisdom (n.)
Philadelphia - city of brotherly love (n.)
audiophile - lover of sound (n.)

49. against- contra

contrary - against something (adj.)
contradict - speak against something (v.)
controversial - ideas against each other (adj.)

50. dict - say

diction - the way something is said (n.)
dictation - the writing of what is said (n.)
dictator - leader who has the only say (n.)

51. against - anti

antibiotic - against a living virus
antibody - fights against disease
anti - Semitic - against Hebrews (adj.)

52. from - de

deduct - subtract from (v.)
degrade - take worth from (v.)
defile - take purity from (v.)

53. God - theo

theology - study of God (n.)
theocracy - government in which God rules (n.)
theism - belief in God (n.)

54. world - cosmo

cosmology - study of the origin of the world (n.)
cosmography - description of the world (adj.)
cosmopolitan - relating to the whole world (adj.)

55. false - pseudo

pseudonym - false name (n.)
pseudoscience - false science (n.)
pseudo - intellectual - false intellectual (n.

56. earth - ge

geography - study of the places of the earth (n.)
geology - study of the elements of the earth (n.)
geothermal - heat of the earth (adj.)

57. macro - large

macrocosm - the universe (n.)
macroscopic - seen without a microscope (adj.)
macrobiotic - promoting long life by diet (adj.)

58. micro - small

microcosm - small world (n.)
microorganism - small organism (n.)
microsecond - one millionth of a second (n.)

59. manu - hand

manuscript - handwriting (n.)
manually - by hand (adj.)
manual - handbook (n.)

60. order- mand

mandate - an order (n.)
mandatory - commanded (adj.)
command - order (n. or v.)

61. soph - wise

sophisticated - worldly-wise (adj.)
sophomore - wise fool, over-confident (n.)
philosophy - love of wisdom (n.)

62. arch - chief

anarchy - without a chief (n.)
archangel - chief angel (n.)
archenemy - chief enemy (n.)
archrival - chief rival (n.)
architect - chief builder (n.)

63. beyond - extra

extracurricular - beyond the curriculum (adj.)
extravagant - beyond the budget (adj.)
extreme - beyond normal (adj.)

64. bi - two

bikini - two piece bathing suit (n.)
bicycle - two - wheel cycle (n.)
bigamy - having two wives (n.)

65. self - auto

autobiography - self-written life story (n.)
automobile - self-moving vehicle (n.)
automatic - operating by itself (adj.)

66. cide - kill

suicide - killing oneself (n.)
genocide - killing a group of people (n.)
insecticide - killing insects (n.)
infanticide - killing of infants (n.)

67. around - peri

perimeter - measurement around (n.)
periphery - the edge around (n.)
periscope - instrument for seeing around (n.)

68. per - through

permeate - soak through (v.)
perspire - lose water through pores (v.)
perforate - put holes through (v.)

69. hydra - water

hydrant - holds water (n.)
dehydrate - remove water from (v.)
hydraulic - powered by water (adj.)

70. aqua - water

aquarium - holds water and fish (n.)
aquamarine - color of water (n.)
aqualunger - scuba diver (n.)
aquatic - relating to water (adj.)

71. semi - half

semi-retired - half-retired (adj.)
semisweet - half-sweet (adj.)
semi-annual - every half year (adj.)
semi-circle - half-circle (n.)

72. hemi - half

hemisphere - half of the world (n.)
hemiplegic - half-paralyzed (adj.)
hemicycle - half a cycle (n.)

Exercise 1 - Choose the best word to go in the blank and circle it.

1. The head city is the _____.
   a. capitol   b. capital   c. metropolis
2. The doctor gave her a _____ to keep her calm.
   a. stimulant   b. depressant   c. sedative
3. Every day they _____ around the drinking fountain.
   a. congregate   b. combine   c. collaborate
4. He measures atmospheric pressure with a _____.
   a. speedometer   b. temperature   c. barometer
5. The author uses a _____ to protect his privacy.
   a. homonym   b. pseudonym   c. anonymous
6. The roads _____ at the corner.
   a. compact   b. conjunction   c. converge
7. Don't be _____ towards your parents.
   a. pandemic   b. gregarious   c. obstinate
8. The "cure-all" is a false _____.
   a. panacea   b. dynasty   c. digress
9. He wrote his own _____ when he was 95 years old.
   a. biology   b. biography   c. autobiography
10. The _____ came in through the window.
    a. dynamo   b. projectile   c. psyche
11. Will you measure the _____ of the circle?
    a. circumscribe   b. mediator   c. circumference
12. The angles are _____.
    a. isogonic   b. dynamic   c. pandemic
13. Look at the fingerprint with a _____.
    a. periscope   b. microscope   c. telescope
14. Our enemy is too _____.
    a. sedentary   b. fraternal   c. aggressive
15. He shows _____ behavior when he screams.
    a. aberrant   b. psychiatry   c. psychology
16. A powerful family or _____ rules the small country.
    a. matriarch   b. theocrat   c. dynasty
17. We don't know who wrote it because it is _____.
    a. extra-terrestrial   b. anonymous   c. controversial
18. The machine broke so we finished the job _____.
    a. internally   b. manually   c. posthumously

19. The antediluvian period _____ the antebellum period.
    a. provides   b. connects   c. antedates
20. Hitler was an anti-Semitic _____.
    a. dictator   b. cosmopolitan   c. anarchist
21. Mother will _____ if the boys start to fight.
    a. aggregate   b. intervene   c. digress
22. They own most of the businesses, so they have a _____.
    a. philosophy   b. monopoly   c. posterity
23. Our _____ father treats us very well.
    a. benevolent   b. portable   c. secluded
24. My secretary must take _____.
    a. cosmography   b. geology   c. dictation
25. The communists attempted _____ in Cambodia.
    a. bigamy   b. monotheism   c. genocide
26. _____ is the study of handwriting.
    a. graphology   b. philosophy   c. manuscript
27. A _____ wants the people to rule.
    a. matriarch   b. democrat   c. theocrat
28. A _____ is a lover of mankind.
    a. philanthropist   b. benediction   c. mediator
29. They always _____ movies before they let their children see them.
    a. predict   b. antedate   c. preview
30. Don't _____ me when I'm talking on the phone.
    a. expire   b. postpone   c. interrupt
31. He joined a _____ because he is gregarious.
    a. monopoly   b. paternity   c. fraternity
32. Please _____ the campfire before you leave.
    a. extinguish   b. expectorate   c. aggregate
33. The disease has become _____.
    a. isothermal   b. hydraulic   c. pandemic
34. The power of heat is called _____.
    a. dynamo   b. thermodynamics   c. geothermal
35. Perfect attendance at school is not _____.
    a. mandatory   b. contrary   c. posterity
36. They will _____ on the project.
    a. perforate   b. dehydrate   c. collaborate

37. He ended his _____ with a benediction.
    a. monologue   b. philosophy   c. anthropology
38. The ancient Egyptians believed in _____.
    a. periphery   b. polytheism   c. anarchy
39. Raisins are _____ grapes.
    a. dehydrated   b. perforated   c. hydrant
40. Having two wives is called bigamy. Having several wives is called _____.
    a. insecticide   b. cosmology   c. polygamy
41. Astrology is a _____.
    a. pseudonym   b. homonym   c. pseudoscience
42. If you want to know the rules, read the _____.
    a. manual   b. dictation   c. lithography
43. The study of the elements of the earth is _____.
    a. geography   b. biography   c. geology
44. She is hard to understand because of her poor _____.
    a. diction   b. theocracy   c. anthropology
45. Do not _____ her by showing her these pictures.
    a. abduct   b. abandon   c. defile
46. A _____ is a small world.
    a. monogamy   b. microcosm   c. macrocosm
47. The _____ loves Beethoven.
    a. audiophile   b. psyche   c. patriarch
48. I will add a _____ to the end of the letter.
    a. post date   b. post script   c. post mortem
49. I cannot _____ through my nose.
    a. expire   b. perforate   c. permeate
50. When she traveled around the world she became very _____.
    a. extracurricular   b. sophisticated   c. mediocre

CROSSWORD PUZZLE

WORD LIST:

AB
ABDUCT
ABERRANT
AN
ANARCHY
BAROMETER
BI
CIRCUMFERENCE
COLONY
COLLABORATE
COMPACT
CONTRA
COSMOS
DE

DECAPITATE
DYNASTY
EX
EXIT
EXPEL
EXTERIOR
GE
HEAD
HEMI
IMPORT
INTERVENE
MANU
MATRIARCH
MONOGAMY
OB
ONE

ONYM
PANORAMA
PATRIARCH
PRE
PSEUDONYM
PSYCHE
RE
REJECT
SAME
SAY
SE
SECEDE
SEE
SOPH
TELE
THERMODYNAMIC

ACROSS

1. capit
5. carry away from
7. throw away
8. against
9. mono
10. worlds
14. false name
15. having one spouse
16. name
20. cut off the head
23. hand
25. measures atmospheric pressure
29. view of all things
31. carry in
32. homo
33. vid
34. again
35. a father who rules a family
38. go out
39. before
40 come between
41. power of heat
44. a group living together

DOWN

1. half
2. powerful family
3. move apart from something
4. earth
5. away from
6. squeezed together
11. dict
12. without a chief or ruler
13. work together
17. two
18. far off
19. outside
21. measure around a circle
22. without
24. away from normal
26. wise
27. a mother who rules a family
28. against
30. mind or soul
36. push out
37. apart
42. out
43. from

Abraham was a patriarch.

GRAMMAR CHALLENGE

After you have finished this book , you should be able to do the following:

1. Write a two - word sentence in present tense using a pronoun and a verb. (p. 2, 11, 14)
2. Change it to past tense. (p. 11)
3. Change it back to present tense and add an article (a, an, the) and change the pronoun to a plural common noun. (p. 8, 11, 14, 39)
4. Add an adjective. (p. 19)
5. Add an adverb. (p. 23)
6. Add a prepositional phrase. (p. 28)
7. Rewrite it as a question. (p. 11)
8. Write a three-word sentence with an apostrophe to show that someone owns something. (p. 26)
9. Change the word with the apostrophe to a possessive pronoun. (p.14)
10. Write a sentence with compound personal pronouns. (p. 17)
11. Write a sentence with a subject, a verb and a direct object. (p. 30)
12. Change the direct object to a plural noun. (p. 39)
13. Add two adjectives to describe the plural noun. (p. 39)
14. Write a sentence using items in a series. (p. 42)
15. Write a sentence using three irregular verbs. (p. 35)
16. Write a sentence with two independent clauses joined by **and** or **but**. (p. 43)
17. Write a sentence with an appositive. (p. 44)
18. Write a sentence with two dependent clauses. (p. 43)
19. Write a sentence with three adjectives before a common noun. (p. 8, 45)
20. Write a sentence using direct address and a proper noun. (p. 8, 46)
21. Write a sentence using quotations. (p. 49)
22. Write a sentence with a quote within a quote. (p. 51)
23. Write a sentence with an interrupted quotation. (p. 49, 50)
24. Write a sentence with independent clauses separated by semicolons. (p. 45)
25. Write a sentence containing a date and an address. (p. 42, 47)
26. Write a sentence containing short independent clauses. (p. 47)
27. Write a sentence with an adverb clause at the beginning of the sentence. (p. 44)
28. Write a sentence containing a reflexive pronoun and a book title. (p. 16, 33)
29. Write a sentence containing the names of three religions. (p. 32)
30. Write a dialogue between two people with three sentences. (p. 51)
31. Write a sentence using the prefix **ex** three times. (p. 55)
32. Write a sentence using the prefix **tele** three times. (p. 55)
33. Write a sentence using the prefix **com** three times. (p. 53)
34. Write a sentence using the prefix **inter** three times. (p. 54)
35. Write a sentence using the prefix **re** three times. (p. 56)
36. Change the last sentence to future tense. (p. 11)
37. Write a two - word sentence which is a command. (p. 12)
38. Write a sentence using the same word twice, once as a noun and once as a verb. (p. 10)
39. Write a sentence using two prepositional phrases showing where and when. (p. 28)
40. Write a sentence using two direct objects connected by **and**. (p. 30)
41. Write a sentence with an appositive phrase. (p. 44)
42. Write a sentence with a non - essential clause. (p. 44)
43. Write a sentence using semi-colons to separate groups of words that contain commas. (p. 42)
44. Write a sentence using the root **port** three times. (p. 56)
45. Write a sentence using the prefix **con** three times. (p. 53)

GRAMMAR SONGS

TEACHER'S GUIDE

Kathy Troxel

Most of us learned our alphabet by singing the "ABC Song." The reason this teaching technique works so well is that music is stored in the right side of the brain and words are stored in the left side of the brain. Singing the words brings both sides of the brain into the learning and remembering process. It also brings the body into the learning process because singing is a learned motor skill which requires deep breathing and physical coordination. Singing alters our mood, focuses our attention and increases our retention.

The *Grammar Songs* program utilizes the following principles of learning theory:

FUN - Benjamin Bloom, the famous learning theorist, studied 120 experts and found certain things they all had in common. The most important factor for all of them was their first teacher. Their first teacher made learning FUN. The children were introduced to the subject as a playful activity and learning at this stage was like a game. The first exposure to any subject of study is the most powerful.

RECITATION - Memory experts say that using your own voices increases memory much better than mere silent repetition. That's why when you ask someone to remind you to do something, they probably won't need to.

ASSOCIATION - When you hear a familiar melody, you think of a phrase. When you hear a familiar phrase, you think of the melody which accompanies it. See if you can read this phrase without hearing the accompanying melody - "Happy Birthday to You"... As teachers, we should use every opportunity to associate dry facts with rhyme, rhythm, pictures, stories and patterns.

ORGANIZATION - If material is organized, it is easier to remember. For example, the "Verb Song" is divided into four verses. Each verse teaches a different type of verb. The verses are organized into patterns of rhythm and rhyme. Any time you can see a pattern in material to be memorized, it is easier.

GOALS - The goal of the student is to memorize all 16 "Grammar Songs" and to complete the exercises in order. The short term goal is to learn a new verse every day and to review all the verses learned up to that point every day. Short-term and long-term goals should be achievable, challenging and always rewarded.

FIVE STEPS TO SUCCESS

1. MEMORIZE

When a student can recall information without effort, he is ready to build upon that knowledge. Mnemonic devices such as picture associations, rhymes and songs should be used as much as possible as a shortcut to memorization.

The "Grammar Songs" are organized in a rhyming framework of verses. The short-term goal is to memorize the first verse. Then memorize the second, the third and so on. Students are rewarded for each step of mastery. Concentrate on one song at a time and review the song even after it is memorized. It will go from the short-term to the long-term memory after a period of time.

A third and fourth grade teacher took her entire class through the first 15 songs in four months. The students memorized all the songs, one at a time and then reviewed all the songs weekly, from the beginning of the tape up to what they had learned.

2. UNDERSTAND

After the student has memorized the song, he will be able to identify the correct answers in the exercises which follow each song. This demonstrates his understanding of what he has memorized.

3. APPLY

The writing exercises provide an opportunity for the student to use his own imagination. He looks at the 16 pictures and draws words out of those pictures. For example, after memorizing the "Verb Song," he should be able to look at picture #1 and find words such as: hiking, walking, looking, thinking, leading, following, listening, smelling, feeling, etc.

4. ANALYZE

The GRAMMAR CHALLENGE GAME gives students an opportunity to put material into categories. They can see similarities between different words because they categorize words according to parts of speech.

5. SYNTHESIZE

After students have practiced writing sentences in prescribed forms, they can start creating on their own. They are free to use an interesting variety of sentence structures. They can experiment because they are confident of their own mastery of grammar and punctuation rules.

Recommended Reading

Build Your Brain Power by Arthur Winter, M.D. and Ruth Winter
St. Martin's, New York

You are about to discover methods of teaching grammar that will save your energy, provide fun and entertainment and really teach. Most students find "Grammar Songs" so much fun that they serve as a reward for good behavior at the end of the day. They can also be used in learning centers for those who need remedial help. Poor readers can be encouraged to learn by teaching them one phrase at a time, in rhythm. When the emphasis is on the rhythm rather than the words, students get positive reinforcement rather than negative humiliation for not knowing a word. Choral reading encourages poor readers. Just turn on the tape and let it do the work for you.

There are many ways to use "Grammar Songs" with students. The following ideas have been used successfully with different age groups by various teachers.

1. Verb Song

A. Say the "Verb Song" in rhythm and have students repeat, one phrase at a time. If the concepts are too difficult in verses 2 - 4 , just teach verse 1.
B. Act out the verbs and have students guess what you are doing.
C. Have students copy the song while you play the tape in the background.
D. Play the song several times and invite them to sing along. If you sing it yourself, with the tape, in an uninhibited manner, they will soon follow. It seems that the more people are coaxed to sing, the more shy they become. Just tell them they will learn faster if they sing along, and leave it at that.
E. Play the tape while students are cleaning their desks or doing an art project.
F. Use the tape for a rainy day when you play musical chairs or do aerobics.
G. Give the students one minute to write as many verbs as they can think of. Reward the student who has the most. If you are working with one student, ask him to get over a certain number within one minute. Let the number be hard enough to be a challenge.
H. Have students look at the picture pages. See who can find the most verbs in each picture within three minutes. Use other pictures for the same exercise.
I. Have students write down all verbs from a story they have read. To make it easier, have them write down all verbs that end in "d." Ex: landed, ended, filled, wanted, etc.
J. Cover some words on the "Verb Song" poster with post it notes. Have a contest to see who can say it with some words missing. Gradually cover up more and more until students can say the whole thing from memory.
K. Give a test on the song by writing just the first letter of each word on the board and let them fill in the blanks.

2. Noun Song

A. Use any of the steps that you used successfully for the "Verb Song." Have students write down all the proper nouns from a story they have read. After they have a list of verbs which end in "d" and nouns, they should be able to rewrite the story in their own words using at least half of the words on their verb and noun lists.
B. Have students write as many common nouns as they can think of in one minute. Have students write as many proper nouns as they can think of in one minute.
C. Have students write as many words as they can think of that are both nouns and verbs. Example: love, brush, usher, reward, etc.

3. Sentence Song

A. Write this sentence on the board. - Tom sees.
Ask the students if it is a sentence. Many of them will say no because they think it is too short. Ask them if it has a noun. They will tell you it is "Tom." Tell them "Tom" is the subject. Ask them if it has a verb. They will tell you it is "sees." Tell them it is a sentence because it has a subject and the subject is doing something. Ask them what the subject is doing. They will say "seeing."
B. Have the students write two-word sentences for each of the pictures. Example: Boys hike. She runs. Pat blows. She skates. They drive.
C. Have them rewrite the sentences in past tense. Example: Boys hiked. She ran. Pat blew. She skated. They drove.
D. Substitute either a question mark or an exclamation point at the end of each sentence to show that they can change the inflection of the sentence by changing the punctuation.
E. Add the word "will" to each sentence to put it into the future tense.
F. After learning the "Sentence Song," have students write a question, a statement and an exclamation for each picture in present, past and future tenses.
G. Have students bring in examples of incomplete sentences used in advertising. Example : Never had it. Never will.
H. Have students copy a paragraph from a story and change the tense to future or present.

4. Pronoun Song

A. Have students write or say sentences for each picture using possessive pronouns.
 Example: Their backpacks are heavy. The skateboard is hers.
B. Have students write or say sentences for each picture using indefinite pronouns.
Example: All of them are singing. Someone is bowling No one understands him.
C. Have students write or say sentences for each picture using reflexive pronouns.
Example: They woke themselves up early for the trip. She taught herself to ride.

5. Compound Personal Pronoun Song

A. Say or write the first two sentences of each verse. Have them finish the verse from memory.
B. Have students substitute their own names for the ones in the song and sing it that way.

6. Adjective Song

A. Have students write as many adjectives as they can think of for each of the pictures.
B. Have students write as many proper adjectives as they can think of . Example: French perfume, Spanish leather, Australian wool, Hawaiian coconuts, Italian opera, etc.
C. Have students list all the adjectives they can find in a story.
D. Expand the exercise on p. 21 by having students add two or more adjectives to the beginning of each sentence.
E. Have students write a sentence for each picture using the Noun - Verb - Adjective pattern. Example: #2 The girl is frightened.
F. Give each student a sheet of paper containing as many adjectives as there are students in

the class. Have them cut up that sheet into that many pieces. Give each student an envelope with the name of another student on it. Instruct them to put one adjective into that student's envelope. They pass the envelopes around the room. Don't allow them to read the contents of the envelope until the end. By the end, every student should have an envelope full of compliments. Use words like: friendly, helpful, generous, punctual, thoughtful, smart, hard-working, patient, athletic, humble, unique, etc.

7. Adverb Song

A. Have students write a sentence for each picture starting with two adverbs.
Example: #4 - Softly and sweetly, the choir is singing.
B. Have students write a sentence for each picture using an adverb phrase at the beginning.
Example #3 .
When - At three o'clock, Don is celebrating.
Where - At his friend's house, Don is celebrating.
How - With great enthusiasm, Don is celebrating.
To what extent - All night long, Don is celebrating.

8. Apostrophe Song

A. Have students write a singular possessive and plural possessive for each picture. Example: boy's backpack - boys' backpacks, girl's scream - girls' screams, man's cake - men's cakes, child's song - children's songs, etc. (Note - the few plural nouns that do not end in *s* form the possessive by adding an apostrophe and an *s*.)
B. Have students find all the apostrophes in a story which show ownership and find the object owned.

9. Preposition Song

A. Have students find and write all the prepositional phrases in a story. Explain that a prepositional phrase is the same as an adverb phrase.
B. Have students write a sentence for each picture beginning or ending with a prepositional phrase. Example : Early in the morning, the boys started their hike.

10. Direct Object Song

A. After the students have learned the "Direct Object Song" and understand the difference between a direct object and prepositional phrase, you can teach them about indirect objects. In the sentence, "I gave him the money," *money* is the direct object and *him* is the indirect object. If the words *to* and *for* are used in the sentence, the word following them is not an indirect object, but part of the prepositional phrase. Example : I gave the money to him (no indirect object) The indirect object always comes before the direct object and answers the question "to whom?" or "for whom?"
B. Have students write or say a sentence for each picture using an indirect object and a direct object. Example: I gave them a map. I gave her a scare. I gave him a cake. They taught me a song.

11. Capital Song

A. Have students make a list of examples for each category.

B. Have a contest to see who can come up with the most organizations or special events in 3 minutes.

C. Have students circle all capitalized words on a page of newspaper and write the rule which applies to each one.

12. Irregular Verb Drill

A. After students have drilled part 1, give them just the infinitives and have them write or say the other forms of the verbs.

B. Have students write a sentence for each irregular verb in past tense.

13. Plural Song

A. Have students find other examples of words which fit into each category. Example: elf - elves, half-halves, calf-calves, shelf-shelves, handkerchief-handkerchieves/handkerchiefs, etc.

14. Comma Song

A. Have students circle all the commas on a page of a newspaper and say the rule which applies to each one.

15. Quotation Mark

A. Using this pattern, have students fill in the dialogue for each picture.
" I want to (verb)," said (proper noun), " and then you can (verb / phrase)."

B. Using the same pattern as above, eliminate the punctuation. Give it as a test to see if they put the commas, periods and quotation marks in the right places.

16. Greek and Latin Prefix and Suffix Song

A. A group of junior high students memorized this song and took a test on it in one period. The 72 Greek and Latin prefixes, suffixes and roots will help them to expand their vocabularies. It is also helpful for college entrance vocabulary exams.

B. Play the song about 15 times or until most of them think they know it. Reward those who can say verse 1, 2, etc. Give a test at the end of the period by writing just the word on the left on the board. They write the word or prefix on the right.

C. Teach the following words for the prefixes and suffixes in section 1: misunderstand, astronaut, object, sedative, democrat, anonymous, homonym, capitol, combine, converge, collect, thermometer.

D. Give a matching test with those words and their definitions. After they have mastered them, choose another word for each prefix/suffix from the list or from the dictionary.

E. When they have mastered section 1, go on to section 2 and so on.

17. The list of nouns, verbs, adjectives and adverbs at the back of the book can be used as a test. Give one form of the word and have students write the other three forms. Have students write sentences using the different forms. Explain that the verbs usually have the word "to" in front of them and the nouns usually have the word "the" in front of them.

GRAMMAR CHALLENGE GAME

After students have become familiar with the parts of speech and punctuation rules, they will enjoy playing this game.

HOW TO PLAY

1. Write the first sentence on the board.

2. Before you start the game, have the students name the part of speech for each word in the sentence. Since the *Grammar Songs* book does not cover articles and conjunctions, list the articles (*a, an* and *the*) and the conjunctions (*and, but, or, nor, for, yet, either-or, neither-nor, both*) on the board. After this review, erase the parts of speech from beneath the words of the sentence.

Example: The   tall,   red-haired   girl   is   sitting
ARTICLE ADJECTIVE ADJECTIVE NOUN LINKING VERB VERB

and   reading   quietly   on   the   sofa.
CONJUNCTION VERB ADVERB PREPOSITION ARTICLE NOUN

3. Divide the group into teams or play one on one.

4. Write the rules on the board.

5. Choose which team goes first by flipping a coin. If the first player on the first team makes a mistake, the turn goes to the other team. Each team gets one point for each correct answer. The team that has the most points at the end of the time limit is the winner. Another way to play is to determine the number of points to be reached ahead of time. The team that reaches that number first is the winner.

RULES

1. All words must be spelled correctly.
2. All sentences must be punctuated correctly, including proper use of capital letters.
3. All sentences must make sense.
4. If anyone talks during someone else's turn, his team loses a point.

TIPS

This game can be easily modified for younger or less advanced students. Allow students to use their books or folders for reference. Repeat the easier instructions as many times as necessary for the majority of the group to catch on. For example, "Change the noun," can be repeated many times until everyone knows what the noun is. The key is to make sure that the instructions are easy enough for most players to get the correct answer most of the time. Write sentences on the board that are appropriate for the players.

GAME 1

The tall, red-haired girl is sitting and reading quietly on the sofa.

1. Change a verb.
2. Change two verbs.
3. Change all the verbs.
4. Change the first noun.
5. Change the second noun.
6. Change the first adjective.
7. Change the second adjective.
8. Change the adverb.
9. Change the preposition.
10. Change the linking verb to past tense.
11. Add a helping verb and change the sentence to future tense.
12. Change two words in the prepositional phrase.
13. Change the nouns to their plural forms and change the linking verb.
14. Add an adjective to describe the second noun.
15. Add quotation marks to the sentence and add two words. Change a period to a comma.

GAME 2

During the movie, he and she are drinking, eating and laughing.

1. Change the first pronoun.
2. Change the second pronoun.
3. Change the adverb.
4. Change the noun.

5. Change a verb.
6. Change two verbs.
7. Add an adverb.
8. Add an adverb to each verb.
9. Change the pronouns to proper nouns.
10. Change the linking verb to past tense.
11. Change the sentence to future tense.
12. Add an adjective to describe the first noun.
13. Change the preposition.
14. Change two words in the prepositional phrase.
15. Change the sentence into a question by adding a question word.

GAME 3

"The bike is theirs," Tom replied, "but you can ride it until they come back."

1. Change the first noun.
2. Change the possessive pronoun.
3. Change the proper noun to a pronoun.
4. Make the first noun plural and change the linking verb.
5. Change the preposition.
6. Add an adjective to describe the noun.
7. Add a prepositional phrase to the end of the sentence.
8. Add a proper noun and a conjunction.
9. Add a conjunction and a possessive pronoun.
10. Add another sentence using quotation marks.
11. Add another sentence using quotation marks and an apostrophe.
12. Add another sentence using quotation marks and interrupted by, "he said."
13. Add another sentence using the title of a song.
14. Add another sentence using an appositive or an appositive phrase.
15. Add another sentence with an address and a date.

GAME 4

Finish the paragraphs using the following sentences as your topic sentences.

There are several ways to have fun at the beach.

1. In the early morning, it's fun to (finish the sentence)
2. After that you can usually (finish the sentence)
3. If the waves are big enough, you can (finish the sentence)
4. When the water gets too cold, (finish the sentence)

5. If the sand is too hot, you can (finish the sentence)
6. Most people enjoy (finish the sentence)
7. The best part of the day is (finish the sentence)

If I had a million dollars to spend, I'd divide it up.

1. First I would (finish the sentence)
2. Then I would (finish the sentence)
3. After that (finish the sentence)
4. If I had the time, I would (finish the sentence)
5. With part of the money, I would (finish the sentence)
6. With another part of the money, I would (finish the sentence)
7. The rest of the cash would be spent on (finish the sentence)
8. Finally, (finish the sentence)

ANSWERS

PAGE 5

Exercise 1

1. should stay, gets
2. may give, finish
3. will throw
4. does play, did
5. have seen
6. did eat, left, are
7. can have, want
8. has gone, gets
9. could send, call
10. had seen, knew, expect

Exercise 2

1. will be, leaves
2. should be, rings
3. would be, could open
4. can be, want, be, am
5. was, lost
6. was, does, yell
7. is, studying
8. am, walk
9. is being
10. are, coming, are, going, stay

Exercise 3

has, mowing, takes, rakes,
puts, picks, mows, is finished,
sweeps, feeds, pay, is finished,
likes

PAGE 9

Exercise 1

Person - doctor, friend, child,
nurse, stranger, man, sister,
fireman

Place - store, park, wall, yard,
zoo, floor, sky, library, bedroom

Thing - flashlight, piano, desk,
book, shirt, pants, guitar, money

Idea - pride, freedom, love,
greatness, friendship, greed

PAGE 10

Exercise 2

1. N, 2. V, 3. V, 4. N, 5. N, 6. V,
7. V, 8. N, 9. V, 10. N, 11. V, 12. N,
13. N, 14. V, 15. V, 16. N, 17. V,
18. N, 19. N, 20. V

PAGE 11

Exercise 1

#1,3,5,6,7,10

PAGE 12

Exercise 3

1. a. baked b. Joseph
2. a. have written b. Liz and
Theresa
3. a. practiced b. musician
4. a. speak = verb b. they = subject
5. a. hid = verb
b. Corrie ten Boom = subject

PAGE 15

Exercise 1

1. she 2. They 3. She, he 4. It
5. them

Exercise 2

1. A 2. B 3. B 4. A
5. B 6. A 7. A 8. B

PAGE 16

Exercise 3

1. his 2. theirs 3. yours. 4. Hers
5. Ours 6. mine 7. its 8. hers
9. ours 10. Yours

Exercise 4

1. Everyone 2. All 3. another
4. Either 5. most 6. No one 7.
Many
8. Someone 9. Several 10. None

Exercise 5

1. himself 2. himself. 3. herself
4. ourselves 5. themselves
6. yourselves 7. yourself 8. itself
9. herself 10. myself

PAGE 18

1. me 2. me 3. her, me 4. me 5. me
6. He, I 7. I 8. me 9. he, me 10. me
11. They, I 12. him, me 13. her, me
14. I 15. us 16. me 17. I
18. She, him, them 19. we 20. her,
him
21. them, us 22. he, she 23. she, he
24. I 25. I, her 26. him 27. her, me
28. I, she 29. She, I 30. we, her

PAGE 22

Exercise 1

1. seventeen 2. black, old 3. silly
4. ferocious, fearful 5. three 6.
easy, chocolate 7. windy
8. tall, dark, handsome, friendly,
strong
9. kind 10. wise, wise

Exercise 2

1. crazy, adventurous 2. silly,
foolish 3. simple 4. old, experi-
enced
5. young, energetic 6. tired,
grumpy
7. hard 8. stubborn, proud
9. talkative, vivacious
10. wealthy, generous

PAGE 24

Exercise 1

1. quickly 2. loudly 3. swiftly
4. clearly 5. hard 6. later 7. often
8. everywhere

Exercise 2

1. solid 2. unusually 3. thoroughly
4. extremely 5. dead 6. brilliant
7. overly 8. partially

Exercise 3

1. very 2. too 3. rather 4. somewhat
5. too 6. more 7. most 8. less

PAGE 27

1. Jim's 2. Tom's 3. Tanya's,
doesn't
4. Adams' 5. She'll, comin', roun'
7. shouldn't 8. She's, isn't 9. '92
10. What's, Lisa's 11. It's 12.
Brad's
13. won't 14. She's, he's
15. Rita's, mother's

PAGE 29

Exercise 1

1. at 2. in 3. out 4. for 5. up
6. beyond 7. through 8. from
9. during, under 10. before, to
11. behind, beneath 12. with
13. on 14. in front of 15. across, for

PAGE 30

Exercise 1 (Answers will vary.)

I hit the ball.
I took the money.
I quit smoking.
I shook the mop.
I squeezed the orange.
I loved the baby.
I pleased the teacher.
I shoved the cart.

PAGE 34

1. I, Washington Monument,
Lincoln Memorial
2. She, Mexican
3. Danish, Solvang
4. Before, I, Christian, I, Hindu
5. The, Channel Islands, Santa
Barbara
6. Southeast Asia, Malaysia
7. When, I, New York, I, Statue of
Liberty
8. The, Australia, Indian, Pacific
Oceans
9. One, New England, Massachusetts
10. Two, Easter, Passover
11. The, Olympics, Seoul, Korea
12. The, Civil War, North, South
13. It's, Wonderful, Life, Christmas
14. For, Chinese, Year, Dragon
15. My Aunt Carmen, National
Geographic
16. The, Protestant, Catholic,
Jewish, White House
17. To Kill, Mockingbird,
Maycomb County, Alabama
18. The, Junior Prom, Winter
Carnival
19. I
20. My, Caucasian, Latin
21. We, Chevrolet, Volkswagen,
Ford
22. Our, Fiddler, Roof
23. Our, Democrats, Republicans
24. The, Queen, England, Parliament
25. Constitution, Bill, Rig

PAGE 38

Exercise 1

1. rang 2. fought 3. shook 4.
bought
5. stung 6. sang 7. bled 8. slew
9. drove 10. dove 11. fled 12. sank
13. hung 14. shrank 15. drank
16. fed 17. led 18. swam 19. struck
20. bit 21. broke 22. strove
23. heard 24. spoke 25. sought
26. bound 27. stood 28. wore
29. tore 30. caught 31. taught
32. shone 33. froze

PAGE 40

Exercise 1

1. leaves 2. boxes 3. pianos
4. knives 5. potatoes 6. wolves
7. enemies 8. flies 9. mice
10. selves 11. feet 12. teeth
13. wives 15. oxen 16. children

17. tomatoes 18. selves
19. sopranos 20. heroes 21. spies
22. halves 23. shelves 24. solos
25. lives 26. ladies 27. churches
28. cities 29. theives 30. brushes

PAGE 45

Exercise 1

1. races, nationalities,
2. week, months
5. Afro-American, Caucasian, Hispanic

Exercise 2

1. door; room;
2. outside; too;
3. me; courage;
4. came; saw;
5. hard; hard;

Exercise 3

1. large, shiny
2. single, wide,
3. filthy, torn,
4. lost, dark,
5. Small, shiny, rare,

PAGE 46

Exercise 4

1. doctor, 2. money, 3. soothing,
4. us, 5. go,

Exercise 5

1. James, 2. Suzanne, 3. Margie,
4. Nurse, 5. Mark,

Exercise 6

1. party, Tammy,
2. Bill, speaker,
3. friend, Larry,
4. neighbor, Shawn,
5. Tyler, baby,

Page 47

Exercise 7

1. up, dressed,
2. came, saw,

3. skis, writes, sings,
4. aspiring, liquids,
5. honest, fair,

Exercise 8

1. book, opinion, 2. movie, her,
3. hostages, hope, 4. She, course,
5. documentary, hand,
6. answer, know,

Exercise 9

1. Blvd., Los Angeles,
2. Drive, Savannah,
3. 28, 4,
4. 7, Ave., Washington,
5. Topeka, Lincoln,
6. Friday, 9, Thursday, 15,

PAGE 50

Exercise 1

1. "It is better," he said, "if I leave early."
2. "Are you coming with us," she asked, "or are you staying home?"
3. "I hate messes!" she yelled.
4. "When is the movie going to start?" he asked.
5. "I really don't know," he said, "what I want to do with my life."
6. She said, "It's a good thing that we wore our jackets."
7. "Are you going to eat with us," she asked, "or will you eat after the game?"
8. They screamed, "Fire! Fire!" as loud as they could.
9. "If you do that again" he roared, "you're fired!"
10. She exclaimed, "I found it at last!"

Exercise 2

1. "Climb Every Mountain"
2. "Hope for the Flowers"
3. "cool"
4. "Darkness"
5. "Chicago"
6. "Taxation Without Representation."
7. "All Creatures Great and Small."
8. " Star Spangled Banner"

9. "Dances with Lions."
10. "rad"

PAGE 51

Exercises 3

1. He said, "I never read 'The Night the Bed Fell.' It's a short story."
2. "Do you ever watch 'Little House on the Prairie'?" she asked.
3. She asked, "What poem begins with this line? 'Whose woods these are I think I know.'"
4. She said, "I can't wait to see what happens on 'Another Life.' "
5. He said, "She said, 'It's over.'"
6. He said, "That shirt is 'rad.' 'groovy' and 'cool.' "
7. "Will you sing 'Sunrise, Sunset' at my wedding?" she asked.
8. He announced, "The Oscar winner is 'Dances With Wolves.'"
9. She said, "His exact words were, 'Give me liberty or give me death.'"
10. He asked, "Do you know the second verse of 'America the Beautiful?'"

Page 51

Exercise 4

> Tom said, ...
> "I don't ...
> "Why do ...
> "Haven't you ...
> Tom said, ...
> "Maybe I can," ...

Page 59 - 61

Exercise 1

1. b. 2. c. 3. a. 4. c. 5. b. 6. c. 7. c.
8. a. 9. c. 10. b. 11. c. 12. a. 13. b.
14. c. 15. a.
16. c. 17. b. 18. b. 19. c.
20. a. 21. b. 22. b. 23. a.
24. c. 25. c. 26. a. 27. b.
28. a. 29. c. 30. c. 31. c.

32. a. 33. c. 34. b. 35. a.
36. c. 37. a. 38. b. 39. a.
40. c. 41. c. 42. a. 43. c. 44. a.
45. c. 46. b. 47. a. 48. b.
49. a. 50. b.

P. 64 - GRAMMAR CHALLENGE
(Answers will vary.)

1. I eat.
2. I ate.
3. The dogs ate.
4. The black dogs eat.
5. The black dogs eat first.
6. In the morning, the black dogs eat first.
7. Do the black dogs eat first in the morning?
8. Pat's dog bites.
9. Her dog bites.
10. He and she are related.
11. He likes the donut.
12. He likes the donuts.
13. He likes the long, twisted donuts.
14. We had ham, eggs, juice and biscuits.
15. When we went to the beach, we swam and rode horses.
16. He sent me a letter, but I didn't receive it.
17. Mrs. Hammond, my favorite teacher, will hand out the award.
18. The older you get, the more time flies.
19. He was wearing loose, wrinkled, dirty clothes.
20. Richard, get up.
21. "I'd like more potatoes," said Amy.
22. He said, "Mother said, 'Dinner's ready.'"
23. "If you need anything," offered Dan, "give me a call."
24. That must have been a valuable ring; he offered a large reward.
25. He was born on Mon., July 25, 1988, at 1221 Crest Lane, Tempe, AZ.
26. I wake up, I read the paper, I think about the day ahead and I get dressed.
27. After the party, we cleaned up the mess.
28. She bought herself a copy of Gone With the Wind.
29. There were Moslems, Hebrews and Christians.
30. " Did you eat yet?" asked Martha.
    " No," Sam replied.
    " Well, would you like some popcorn?"
31. Before you exit, extinguish the fire and turn out the exterior light.
32. The television commercial said, "If the telephone doesn't ring, send a telegraph."
33. He communicated the complete message to the committee.
34. Will you interrupt the interview with the international director?
35. During the rehearsal, we reviewed our lines and replaced the scenery.

PAGE 62 - CROSSWORD

36. During the rehearsal, we will review our lines and replace the scenery.
37. Stand up.
38. May I use your brush to brush my hair?
39. In the summer, we will go across the ocean.
40. We ate cheese and crackers.
41. Uncle Frank, my only relative, will be at the performance.
42. Harry Truman, who was vice - president, became the president.
43. We lived at these addresses: 140 E. 5th St., L.A., Ca.; 226 N. Walnut St., N.Y., N.Y.; and 14 S. Rose Ave., Augusta, Ga.
44. When I met him at the airport, I was carrying my portable radio and wearing imported perfume.
45. If we congregate and concentrate we can conquer this problem.

WRITTEN EXERCISES

PAGE 4 (Answers will vary.)
1. hiking, reading, walking, leading, following
2. running, yelling, reaching, pounding, crying
3. counting, wishing, blowing, celebrating, sitting
4. singing, reading, standing, caroling, enjoying
5. bending, smiling, bowling, looking, hoping

6. lighting, burning, smiling, smoking, thinking
7. worrying, wondering, thinking, frowning, wearing
8. riding, moving, bending, balancing, looking
9. looking, drinking, enjoying, sipping, tasting
10. shaking, shivering, chattering, freezing
11. talking, sharing, eating, sitting, giving, taking
12. driving, cruising, speeding, looking, riding
13. listening, discussing, thinking, teaching, learning
14. floating, sunning, tanning, wiggling, relaxing
15. playing, building, sharing, digging, kneeling
16. speeding, riding, racing, leaning, pedaling

PAGE 10 (Answers will vary.)

1. boys, shoes, hats, backpacks, map, rope, socks, shorts
2. heels, pants, arms, eyes, mouth, blouse, hair, tears
3. cake, candles, vest, fire, air, shirt, table, fingers
4. books, songs, hats, scarves, mittens, music, harmony
5. bowling ball, alley, holes, vest, man, shirt, shoes
6. match, fire, smoke, smile, shoes, shorts, trouble
7. man, frown, eyes, tie, jacket, shirt, nose, eyes
8. skateboard, goggles, kneepads, cap, wheels, girl
9. headband, lady, drink, glass, straw, lips, collar
10. snow, float, duck, man, swimsuit, hands, ice, slush
11. grandmother, boy, wheelchair, cookies, table, time
12. van, wheels, smoke, sunglasses, man, woman, design
13. people, leader, students, teacher, chairs, lamp
14. pool, water, sunglasses, tan, boy, float, waves
15. sandcastle, children, flags, sand, swimsuits, summer
16. tricycle, pedals, wheels, boy, grin, dust, handles

PAGE 13 (Answers will vary.)

1. The boys are hiking.
2. The lady is running.
3. The man is blowing.
4. The carolers are singing.
5. The bowler is smiling.
6. The kid is grinning
7. The man is thinking.
8. The girl is riding.
9. The lady is sipping.
10. The fool is shivering.
11. The friends are eating.
12. The couple is driving.
13. The people are listening.
14. The boy is floating.
15. The children are playing.
16. The rider is speeding.

PAGE 21 (Answers will vary.)

1. The teenage boys are hiking.
2. The frightened woman is running.
3. The older man is blowing.
4. The happy carolers are singing.
5. The college student is bowling.
6. The mischievous boy is smiling.
7. The serious man is thinking.
8. The silly girl is skateboarding.
9. The amiable lady is sipping.
10. The crazy man is shivering.
11. The two friends are sharing.
12. The young couple is cruising.
13. The quiet people are listening.
14. The tanned boy is floating.
15. The three children are playing.
16. The little boy is racing.

PAGE 25 (Answers will vary.)

Add the following words to the ends of the sentences on page 21.

1. here
2. fast
3. hard
4. loudly
5. well
6. fiendishly
7. deeply
8. quickly
9. slowly
10. there
11. happily
12. proudly
13. intently
14. peacefully
15. together
16. now

PAGE 30 (Answers will vary.)

I hit the ball.
I took the money.
I quit the job.
I shook the mop.
I squeezed the sponge.
I loved the baby.
I pleased the teacher.
I shoved the cart.

PAGE 31 (Answers will vary.)

1. along the trail.
2. down the street.
3. candles.
4. carols.
5. ball.
6. match.
7. tie.
8. a skateboard.
9. drink
10. in the snow.
11. cookies.
12. van.
13. to the speaker.
14. in the pool.
15. sandcastle.
16. tricycle.

NOUNS	VERBS	ADJECTIVES	ADVERBS
love	love	loving	lovingly
hate	hate	hateful	hatefully
conservation	conserve	conservative	conservatively
imagination	imagine	imaginative	imaginatively
corruption	corrupt	corrupt	corruptly
suggestion	suggest	suggestive	suggestively
anxiety		anxious	anxiously
consideration	consider	considerate	considerately
production	produce	productive	productively
action	act	active	actively
devotion	devote	devoted	devotedly
cooperation	cooperate	cooperative	cooperatively
function	function	functional	functionally
respect	respect	respectful	respectfully
encouragement	encourage	encouraging	encouragingly
care	care	careful	carefully
sadness	sadden	sad	sadly
gladness	gladden	glad	gladly
stiffness	stiffen	stiff	stiffly
toughness	toughen	tough	toughly
mess	mess	messy	messily
life	live	living	lively
rest	rest	restful	restfully
sleep	sleep	sleepy	sleepily
thanks	thank	thankful	thankfully
response	respond	responsive	responsively

NOUNS	VERBS	ADJECTIVES	ADVERBS
strength	strengthen	strong	strongly
beauty	beautify	beautiful	beautifully
glory	glorify	glorious	gloriously
peace	pacify	peaceful	peacefully
creation	create	creative	creatively
prosperity	prosper	prosperous	prosperously
embarrassment	embarrass	embarrassing	embarrassingly
protection	protect	protective	protectively
expectation	expect	expectant	expectantly
description	describe	descriptive	descriptively
temptation	tempt	tempting	temptingly
insistence	insist	insistent	insistently
repetition	repeat	repetitious	repetitiously
completion	complete	complete	completely
satisfaction	satisfy	satisfactory	satisfactorily
criticism	criticize	critical	critically
obedience	obey	obedient	obediently
hesitation	hesitate	hesitant	hesitantly
admiration	admire	admiring	admiringly
thought	think	thoughtful	thoughtfully
intention	intend	intent	intently
energy	energize	energetic	energetically
definition	define	definite	definitely
success	succeed	successful	successfully
progress	progress	progressive	progressively
excitement	excite	excited	excitedly

PROGRESS CHART

	CAN SING ALONG	CAN WRITE FROM MEMORY	CAN SPELL CORRECTLY	COMPLETED EXERCISES	CORRECTED EXERCISES
VERB SONG					
NOUN SONG					
SENTENCE SONG					
PRONOUN SONG					
COMPOUND PERSONAL PRONOUN DRILL	X				
ADJECTIVE SONG					
ADVERB SONG					
APOSTROPHE SONG					
PREPOSITION SONG					
DIRECT OBJECT SONG					
CAPITAL SONG					
IRREGULAR VERB DRILL	X				
PLURAL SONG					
COMMA SONG					
QUOTATION MARK SONG					
GREEK & LATIN PREFIX & SUFFIX SONG					

INDEX